53 KOREAN FOODS
YOU HAVE TO TRY

53 KOREAN FOODS YOU HAVE TO TRY

Hollym

Carlsbad, CA and Seoul

53 KOREAN FOODS YOU HAVE TO TRY

Copyright © 2016 Korean Food Promotion Institute

Project Planning

Project Director Park Chan-su (Hollym Corp., Publishers)

Project Manager Hahm Minji (Hollym Corp., Publishers)

Food and Text Choi Jia (O'ngo Food Communications)

Food Styling Lee Yebin, Kim Ran, Lee Jung Yun (O'ngo Food Communications)

Photo Kim Eun-ju, Yoon Dong-gil (OFFG studio 64)

Design Yong Lee, Lee Seoung-soo (B2)

Editorial Supevisor Kevin L. Vu

First published in 2016
Second printing, 2017
by Hollym International Corp., Carlsbad, CA, USA
Phone 760 814 9880
http://www.hollym.com   **e-Mail** contact@hollym.com

Hollym

Published simultaneously in Korea
by Hollym Corp., Publishers, Seoul, Korea
Phone +82 2 734 5087   **Fax** +82 2 730 5149
http://www.hollym.co.kr   **e-Mail** hollym@hollym.co.kr

ISBN: 978-1-56591-481-0
Library of Congress Control Number: 2016935919

Printed in Korea

Foreword

Definitely the word "health" would be the key word to represent the food culture of the modern world. This phenomenon not only occurs in Korea but also worldwide. However, the concept of "health" is different in every culture and it is revised, according to the times.

Nowadays, the word "health" no longer means replenishing poor nutrition with high-calorie food. Currently the concept of health has changed from "abundant amount of nutrition" to the "right amount of nutrition." Thus, the Korean Food Promotion Institute has published a book called *53 Korean Foods You Have to Try* which introduces variety of Korean foods that are easy to make and rich in nutrition. Recipes that are introduced in this book are quite simple and straightforward. For those who are trying to make Korean food for the first time, one will find the recipes easy to prepare.

Most of Korean foods are healthy and rich in nutrition, which can be definitely enjoyed by people from all over the world. Therefore, by writing this book, we hope more people become more aware of Korean food and will enjoy it.

March 2016
Korean Food Promotion Institute

Preface

The menus that are selected to be published in this book are based on foods that are representations and characteristics of Korean cuisine. The recipes are healthy and simple to prepare.

It is not difficult to make Korean food at home with seasonal ingredients, if you have basic seasoning. For those attempting to make Korean food for the first time, one may find the preparation process of chopping and mincing, the ingredients difficult. However, once the ingredients are ready, the cooking method is quite simple and straightforward. It does not take a long time.

This book is divided into seven sections and each section is organized by the main ingredients. Moreover, any kind of chemical or artificial seasoning (e.g. MSG) is not included in the recipe. One can then enjoy the true, Korean flavour and original taste of the ingredients.

All the menus that are introduced in this book are simple and straightforward. For those who are trying to make Korean food for the first time, one can easily prepare the recipes without any difficulties. Also, most of the ingredients that are introduced in this book are easily found in almost every grocery store. Moreover, one can adjust the level of spiciness and saltiness of the seasoning to one's taste.

The recipes in this book are healthy, delicious, and simple. We wish and hope more people will be able to enjoy Korean food.

Contents

Foreword 5

Preface 7

Introduction 10

The Basis of Hansik, Korean Food 20

Myeolchi-yuksu Anchovy Stock 22

So-gogi-yuksu Beef Stock 26

Chaeso-yuksu Vegetable Stock 30

Vegetable Dishes Rich in Dietary Fiber 34

Ssam-bap Leaf Wraps and Rice 36

Oi-saengchae Cucumber Salad 40

Mu-saengchae Radish Salad 44

Kong-namul-muchim Seasoned Bean Sprouts 48

Dotori-muk-muchim Acorn Jelly Salad 52

Beoseot-bokkeum Stir-fried Assorted Mushrooms 56

Sigeumchi-namul Seasoned Spinach 60

Hobak-namul Seasoned Zucchini 64

Japchae Stir-fried Glass Noodles and Vegetables 68

Yeondubu Silken Tofu Salad 72

Dubu-jorim Braised Tofu in Soy Sauce 76

Nokdu-bindae-tteok Mung Bean Pancake 80

Bibim-guksu Spicy Noodles 84

Kong-guksu Noodles in Cold Soybean Soup 88

Gamja-sujebi Potato Hand-pulled Dough Flakes Soup 92

Sundubu-jjigae Soft Tofu Stew 96

Seafood Dishes Packed with Iron and Mineral 100

Godeungeo-jorim Braised Mackerel 102

Ojingeo-bokkeum Stir-fried Squid 106

Myeolchi-bokkeum Stir-fried Anchovies 110

Kkotge-tang Spicy Blue Crab Stew 114

Miyeok-guk Seaweed Soup 118

Haemul-pajeon Seafood and Green Onion Pancake 122

Good Sources of Protein, Meat and Egg Dishes 126

Bulgogi Bulgogi 128

Galbi-gui Grilled Beef Ribs 132

Galbi-jjim Braised Short Ribs 136

Dak-galbi Spicy Stir-fried Chicken 140

Dak-gangjeong Fried Chicken with Flavored Soy Sauce 144

Jjim-dak Braised Chicken in Soy Sauce 148

Samgyetang Ginseng Chicken Soup 152

Bossam Kimchi Wraps with Pork 156

Jaeyuk-bokkeum Stir-fried Pork 160

Pyogobeoseot-jeon Shiitake Mushroom Pancake 164

Gyeran-jjim Steamed Eggs 168

Yukgaejang Spicy Beef Soup 172

Gluten-free, Rice and Rice Dishes 176

Ssal-bap Cooked White Rice 178

Chaeso-gimbap Vegetable Gimbap 182

Bibimbap Bibimbap 186

Kimchi-bokkeum-bap Kimchi Fried Rice 190

Hobak-juk Pumpkin Porridge 194

Tteokguk Sliced Rice Cake Soup 198

Tteok-bokki Stir-fried Rice Cake 202

A Gold Mine of Vitamins,
Kimchi and Fermented Foods 206

Baechu-kimchi Kimchi 208

Oi-sobagi Cucumber Kimchi 212

Kkakdugi Diced Radish Kimchi 216

Geot-jeori Fresh Kimchi (Korean Salad) 220

Kimchi-jeon Kimchi Pancake 224

Dubu Kimchi Stir-fried Kimchi with Tofu 228

Kimchi-jjigae Kimchi Stew 232

Doenjang-jjigae Soybean Paste Stew 236

Nutritious Snacks and Desserts
That Boost Your Happiness 240

Sujeonggwa Cinnamon Punch 242

Patbingsu Korean Shaved Ice with Sweet Red Bean 246

Hotteok Pan-fried Sweet Pancake 250

Yaksik Sweet Rice with Nuts and Jujubes 254

Index 258

Ingredients

The recipes in this book offer you easy, delicious, and popular ways Koreans cook and season their fresh seasonal ingredients. Below are the essential and useful sauces and ingredients for you to try out these recipes.

Gochutgaru (Red chilli flakes)

Taeyangcho, meaning sun-dried red chilli, is very popular for cooking in Korea. Red chilli is ground at different degrees according to the purpose of cooking. Finely ground chilli flakes are used for making red chilli paste and a seasoning sauce. Regular ground chilli flakes are for making kimchi, while roughly ground ones are used for summer kimchi like young radish kimchi. Fresh, red, and newly ground chilli flakes can give a more "flavourful spicy taste." In order to maintain their flavour and aroma, chilli flakes should be sealed and kept in a cool place.

Gochujang (Red chilli paste)

Gochujang is Korean traditional fermented condiment, made from glutinous rice or wheat, red chilli flakes, malt, fermented soybean powder, and salt. It is full of nutrients and capsaicin that gives *gochujang* a spicy taste stimulates your appetite and promotes digestion. This spicy seasoning is usually made around in March when it is not warm yet. These days, more people purchase it rather than make it at home. *Gochujang* products usually indicate the level of spiciness on its label, so you can choose the right level depending on your taste.

Ganjang (Soy sauce)

Ganjang has been a popular seasoning for Korean dishes. This salty flavoured light black liquid is made by soaking lumps of fermented soybeans in brine for 30 to 40 days and then simmering the water. *Ganjang* is mainly divided into *gukganjang* (light soy sauce) and *jinganjang* (dark soy sauce). While *gukganjang* tastes saltier and mostly used for seasoning stews or soups, *jinganjang* is richer and less salty and used for seasoning dishes.

Doenjang (Soybean paste)

Doenjang is another major condiment for seasoning various kinds of dishes including *namul,* stews, and soups. After soaking *meju,* lumps of fermented soybeans, is brined for fermentation for 30 to 40 days, the liquid is divided to make *ganjang.* The solid are stored in a separate earthen jar with salt on top to make *doenjang.* Depending on the ingredients added, fermentation time and methods, different kinds of *doenjang* can be created. These days it is made in a simpler way by injecting cooked soybeans with yeast cultivated in either barley or rice, adding salt to it and then leaving it rest for fermentation.

Sikcho (Vinegar)

There are various types of vinegars according to its main ingredients, such as fruit vinegar, cereal vinegar, and synthetic vinegar. Fruit vinegar can be classified into persimmon vinegar, apple vinegar, and wild grape vinegar. Cereal vinegar can be made from rice, brown rice, or barley. Each one has a distinctive flavour, so you can enhance the flavour of dishes by selecting matching vinegar.

Chamgireum (Sesame oil)

Sesame oil is amber coloured oil made by pressing roasted sesame seeds. It is not used as cooking oil because it has low smoking point. Rather it is mainly used as a flavour enhancer because it is quite nutty and aromatic. By adding only a little, it can give dishes extra flavours.

Deulgireum (Perilla or Wild sesame oil)

Perilla oil is very aromatic. It leaves behind a nutty taste when added to a dish. Pressed from roasted perilla seeds, this healthy oil is a wonderful match with cooked vegetable dishes. You can wisely use this beneficial oil by adding it to *namul* dishes or grinding it for salad dressings. Once you buy a bottle of perilla oil, you should keep it in a dark, cool place considering it is easily oxidized.

Mulyeot (Jocheong) / Ssalyeot (Rice syrup)

Rice syrup is used as a sweetener in Korean cuisine. It adds a touch of sweetness and a shiny glaze to dishes. Providing a different kind of sweetness from that of sugar, it is often used for traditional Korean dishes.

Kkaesogeum (Sesame seeds)

When you roast sesame seeds, they have a nuttier flavour and a crispy texture. If you want to enhance the nutty flavour, you can add ground sesame seeds to dishes. If you want to enjoy the crispy texture, you can use them as a garnish to finish dishes.

Buchu (Korean chive)

Korean chive has distinct aroma and flavour, different from those of Western chive. Because of its versatility as an ingredient, it is often used for kimchi filling or *jeon,* pan-fried Korean pancakes. It is also added to fresh salads and topped as a garnish on dishes since it has a garlicky flavour and strong aroma.

Daechu (Jujube or Korean dates)

Korean dates are not only eaten fresh as fruit, but also used dried as an ingredient for dishes. Since dried red *daechu* adds pleasant, gentle sweetness to dishes. It is used as an important ingredient for traditional Korean dishes like *galbijjim* or *dolsot-bap,* cooked rice served in a stone pot.

Kkaennip (Perilla leaf)

Kkaennip is one of the most popular herbs in Korea. As a member of the mint family with strong aroma, it is either many people's favourite herb or the opposite. It is also a versatile ingredient that is used for many Korean dishes including *ssam, jeon,* and *kkaennip-kimchi.*

Saeujeot (Salted shrimp)

Jeot or *jeotgal* is a salty fish sauce made of various kinds of fermented seafood. Each *joetgal* has a distinctive taste and it can play a huge role in defining the taste of a dish. *Saeujeot,* shrimp sauce, is one of the most popular kinds. It is often used for kimchi filling and makes a perfect combination with pork dishes. It gives a savoury flavour and a salty taste to dishes and can be replaced with fish sauce, which is easier to get in hand. High quality shrimp sauce looks bright and shiny and has a clean and mild flavour.

Dangmyeon (Glass noodle)

Glass noodles, *dangmyeon,* are also known as cellophane noodles. They are usually made from sweet potato starch. Korean glass noodles are thicker and dark coloured compared to those used in many Southeast Asian countries. They are cooked until transparent or stir-fried after being soaked in hot water.

Dubu (Tofu)

Tofu is a well-known source of protein as well as a healthy food. It doesn't have any strong flavour or aroma but it comes in many types of textures. That's why you can create a countless varieties of tofu dishes, using different ways of cooking. Tofu is undoubtedly a special food that you never get tired of eating.

Jeongjong/Matsul (Rice wine)

Jeongjong, traditional Korean wine, is a useful ingredient that removes unpleasant smells of fish and meat.

Maesilaek (Plum syrup)

Maesilaek or *maesil* extract has been widely used in Korean cuisine as a sweetener and tea. At the beginning of summer, when plums are still green, you are ready to make *maesilaek*. Green plums and sugar are stacked in a jar and left in a cool, dry place for more than 100 days. When fermented enough, this plum syrup can be used to spice up dishes or added to water for tea or iced tea.

Korean-Style Eating

A daily Korean meal consists of rice, side dishes mainly made of vegetables and either a soup or a stew. These three essentials fulfil our basic nutritional requirements. Regardless of which region we are from, steamed rice and *banchan*(Korean side dishes) are essential to the daily diet. We try not to repeat ingredients that are used in *banchan* either in a soup or a stew. Koreans like to give a variety of flavours and texture to dishes by using fresh seasonal ingredients or dried and then rehydrated vegetables.

On special occasions, rare seasonal ingredients such as abalone, croaker, are added to make special side dishes. Unlike in the West, where the nutritional value of food is measured in calories, in Korea the process of eating and the combination of ingredients keeps us in good health. All the dishes including the cooked rice, a stew and side dishes are served at once. Thus, you can enjoy various kinds of flavour depending on the way you combine the dishes.

There are yin and yang in Korean food and according to this belief, a person's body is healthy only when the yin-yang is in balance. If you have seen Koreans eating hot *samgyetang* (ginseng chicken soup) in summer you might have wondered, "Why do Koreans have hot *samgyetang* in the middle of the summer?" From the perspective of oriental philosophy, it is believed that during the summer, the yang energy travels outward from our body while the yin energy stays deep inside our bodies cool. *Samgyetang,* is an energizing soup-based dish and is traditionally served during the summer for its nutrients, which can easily be lost through excessive sweating and physical exertion during the hot summer. In every Korean meal there has to be a harmonious balance between taste and nutrition. Rather than focusing on individual ingredients or dish, we think about a meal as a whole-combination is integral to our eating style.

Table setting for Korean food is rather simple. Regardless of the menus, a spoon and a pair of chopstick are placed with all the dishes. Since most of the side dishes, except for two bowls of rice and a soup, are shared and small individual plates are provided to each person. In the past, Korean ancestors used different types of kitchenware for different seasons to enjoy the beauty of the four seasons.

The Confucian values had a strong influence in Korean eating culture. When people of different ages and genders eat together, it is polite for the younger people to wait for the eldest to start eating. Even when pouring or receiving a drink, you should politely hold the bottle or the glass with both hands. When you drink at a formal occasion or at a meal with elders, it is polite to slightly turn to your right with the glass in your hands and then drink it.

Although some of the older traditions have relaxed in recent days, there are Korean table manners still in use today. First, wait for the oldest person to sit down first before you take a seat at the table. Second, before you eat, it is polite to say that you are looking forward to the meal. In Korean, people say "jalmukesumnida." Third, during the meal, don't hold the bowl of soup or rice. Also during the meal, don't blow your nose at the table. If someone has hosted you in their home or treated you to a meal out, it is customary to acknowledge your thanks after the meal. In Korea, people say "masigaemugeotsumnida."

Menu Planning for Korean Food

The most important feature of Korean Cuisine is the seasonal and quality of the ingredients. It is also important to know where all the ingredients are grown or sourced. Some vegetables and fruits are available seasonally. Consuming these vegetables and fruits makes one aware and appreciate the changing seasons.

The basic menus to make Korean food are cooked rice, a couple of side dishes, which includes kimchi and a soup or a stew. Kimchi is a traditional Korean dish made of seasoned vegetables and salt. Koreans eat it at nearly every meal. It can be fresh, like a salad, or it can be fermented. While the most popular variety is spicy kimchi made of cabbage, there are hundreds of different types of kimchi made of different vegetables, and not all of them are spicy.

Besides rice, the staples of Korean cooking are vegetables, meat, fish, seafood and tofu. Ideally, a meal mainly includes vegetables and protein based side dishes such as meat or fish. For a vegetarian diet, you can simply replace the protein based dishes for beans or tofu based dishes. Korean vegetarian diet helps you to fulfill your nutritional needs. It is recommended that 70% is vegetable based dishes and 30% is protein and carbohydrate based dishes.

The essence of Korean cuisine is creating a balance between ingredients flavors, colors and cooking techniques to produce a well-balanced and tasty meal. What's so unique about a Korean meal is that you can fulfill your nutritional needs in one meal, and helps you to stay healthy.

Choosing Dinnerware for Korean Food

For rice and a soup, small-sized bowls are usually used for each person. Traditionally plates were used at banquets, and small bowl-shaped plates were used for everyday table settings. Korean ancestors enjoyed and tasted the beauty of different seasons by using sets of brassware during the cold winter and porcelain ware during the warm spring and summer. Koreans don't strictly keep these rules any longer, but for formal occasions, it is advisable to use sets of dinnerware in the same colour and material and steel spoons and chopsticks.

What to Drink with Korean Food

In Korea, there are various ways to set the tables for different occasions. Traditionally, all different types of table settings have its own name: *Ban-sang* (a table for cooked rice and side dishes), *Myeong-sang* (a table for noodle dishes), *Cha-sang* or *Dagua-sang* (a table for tea and snacks like *tteok* or *hangwa*, Korean traditional cookies) and *Juan-sang* (a table for alcoholic drinks and *jeon*, Korean traditional pancake).

Korean restaurants are quite generous with serving water or tea. They usually serve caffeine-free teas such as barley tea or Solomon's seal tea. You can drink it as much as you want.

In Korea, different types of teas are served during and after a meal. Usually unsweetened teas are served during the meal and sweet teas such as *Maesil-cha* (sweet plum tea) and *Yuja-cha* (citron tea) are served after the meal as dessert. There are drinks that go well with certain dishes. Thus, rather choosing a drink based on the flavor of a dish, these are the recommendations that might help you:

Tofu kimchi with *makggeolli* (rice wine)
Meat dishes with *soju*
Maesilju (plum wine) as an aperitif
Bokbunjaju (black raspberry wine) as a digestif

You can also enjoy various kinds of traditional Korean drinks such as *Insamju* (ginseng wine) and *Andong soju* (*soju* made in *Andong*).

The Basis of Hansik, Korean Food

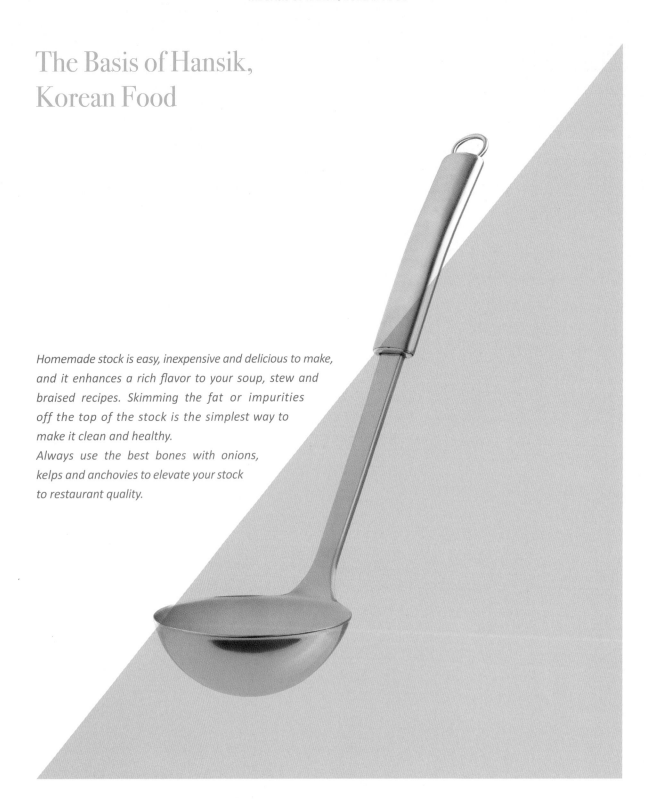

Homemade stock is easy, inexpensive and delicious to make, and it enhances a rich flavor to your soup, stew and braised recipes. Skimming the fat or impurities off the top of the stock is the simplest way to make it clean and healthy.
Always use the best bones with onions, kelps and anchovies to elevate your stock to restaurant quality.

The Basis of Hansik, Korean Food

Myeolchi-yuksu
Anchovy Stock

So-gogi-yuksu
Beef Stock

Chaeso-yuksu
Vegetable Stock

멸
치
육
수

Myeolchi-yuksu

Anchovy Stock

Makes about 10 cups

Ingredients

3 litres (3 qts) cold water

250 g (9 oz) medium or large dried anchovies

1 small onion, trimmed

2 stalks leek, cut into 5 cm (2 in) lengths

5 cloves garlic, crushed

30 g (1 oz) dried kelp

3 dried *pyogo* (shiitake) mushrooms

Method

멸치육수

1

Remove the heads and the organs of the dried anchovies.

2

Place all ingredients in a heavy-based pot. Bring to a boil.

Tip

Anchovy stock is important. It is as essential in Korean cuisine as chicken stock is to Western cuisine. The stock is used to make savory stews, soups, and noodle dishes. The key to making a delicious stock is having the quality ingredients such as kelp and quality fish. Large size anchovies are recommended. The stock should be clear with a strong and robust flavor.

Myeolchi-yuksu

3

Remove the kelp. Lower the heat to a gentle simmer.
Skim the surface of the stock with a ladle to remove any impurities.
Keep simmering for 30 minutes.

4

Remove stock from the stove.
Discard the anchovies and vegetables.
Strain the stock. Store in the refrigerator for up to 3 days.

소
고
기
육
수

—

So-gogi-yuksu

Beef Stock

Makes about 10 cups

Ingredients

1 kg (2 lb) beef round or brisket

4 litres (4 qts) water

10 g (⅓ oz) dried kelp

600 g (1 lb 3 oz) white radish

2 stalks leek, cut into 5 cm (2 in) lengths

½ onion, trimmed

10 cloves garlic, crushed

1 tablespoon black peppercorns

So-gogi-yuksu

Method

소
고
기
육
수

1

Trim beef and cut all the vegetables into big chunks.

2

Put all ingredients in a heavy-based big pot. Bring to a boil.

Tip

Stews and soups are part of a Korean meal. Beef stock is the foundation of many soups in Korea. It can be eaten either as a broth or used as a liquid in a delicious soup. When braising meat dishes, the stock adds another depth and dimension. It is simple to make and an essential key element in a Korean kitchen. To make the beef stock, is to invest in one's time and labor.

So-gogi-yuksu

3
Reduce heat to a gentle simmer and cook for 10 minutes.
Remove the kelp. Keep simmering for 1 hour. Skim any impurities.

4
Discard all the ingredients from stock. Strain the stock through
a muslin. Store in the refrigerator for up to 3 days or
in the freezer for 2 months.

채
소
육
수

—

Chaeso-yuksu

Vegetable Stock

Makes about 10 cups

Ingredients

4 litres (4 qts) cold water

600 g (1 lb 4 oz) white radish

2 green chilli peppers (optional)

2 red chilli peppers (optional)

60 g (2 oz) dried kelp

4 dried *pyogo* (shiitake) mushrooms

Chaeso-yuksu

Method

채
소
육
수

1

Put all the ingredients in a heavy-based pot. Bring to a boil.

2

Lower the heat. Simmer for 10 minutes and then take out the kelp.
Keep simmering for another 30 minutes.
Skim the surface with a ladle to remove any impurities.

Tip

A well-made vegetable stock is essential in any kitchen. It can be used in many different dishes such as a braising liquid or in a soup. In this recipe, it is used as a liquid to braise a Korean cooked salad called namul-dishes. It helps to enhance the flavors of the salad. Depending on your taste, add chilli peppers for a spicy kick.

Chaeso-yuksu

3

Remove the stock from the stove. Strain it, using a muslin cloth.
The stock can be stored in the refrigerator for up to 3 days or
in the freezer for 2 months.

Vegetable Dishes Rich in Dietary Fiber

Korean Cuisine is largely based on rice and vegetables. Many dishes especially na-mul -seasoned vegetables- is one of the most loved Korean side dishes. They are low in calories and rich in dietary fiber.

Vegetable Dishes Rich in Dietary Fiber

Ssam-bap
Leaf Wraps and Rice

Oi-saengchae
Cucumber Salad

Mu-saengchae
Radish Salad

Kong-namul-muchim
Seasoned Bean Sprouts

Dotori-muk-muchim
Acorn Jelly Salad

Beoseot-bokkeum
Stir-fried Assorted Mushrooms

Sigeumchi-namul
Seasoned Spinach

Hobak-namul
Seasoned Zucchini

Japchae
Stir-fried Glass Noodles and Vegetables

Yeondubu
Silken Tofu Salad

Dubu-jorim
Braised Tofu in Soy Sauce

Nokdu-bindae-tteok
Mung Bean Pancake

Bibim-guksu
Spicy Noodles

Kong-guksu
Noodles in Cold Soybean Soup

Gamja-sujebi
Potato Hand-pulled Dough Flakes Soup

Sundubu-jjigae
Soft Tofu Stew

<u>01</u>

Ssam-bap

Leaf Wraps and Rice

Serves 4 with steamed rice as a meal

쌈
밥

Ingredients

200 g (7 oz) assorted leafy greens

200 g (7 oz) cabbage, trimmed quartered

1 carrot, cut into sticks

1 cucumber, cut into sticks

4 cups multi grain steamed rice or steamed white rice

Sauce

Dipping sauce

2 tablespoons soybean paste *(doen-jang)*

2 teaspoons chilli paste *(gochu-jang)*

1 teaspoon honey

2 teaspoons garlic, finely chopped

2 teaspoons green onion, finely chopped

½ tablespoon sesame oil

1 teaspoon sesame seeds, crushed

Ssam-bap

Method

1

Mix all ingredients for dipping sauce.

2

Steam cabbage for 15 minutes. Set aside.

3

Arrange the sauce, leafy greens and vegetable sticks.

쌈
밥

Tip | *The freshest lettuces and leaves of all kinds of plants are always available in the country. If you have lots of leafy vegetables, on hand, you are ready to make ssam-bap. Thicker greens like cabbage can be blanched or steamed, while soft greens like lettuce are eaten raw. A delicious dipping sauce for ssam-bap is simple, fresh, and aromatic and easy to make.*

▌ *How to eat*

Ssam-bap

1

Place rice on any leafy green or steamed cabbage.

2

Add some sauce on top.

3

Roll into a wrap and eat.

02

Oi-saengchae

Cucumber Salad

Serves 4-6 as a side dish

Ingredients

300 g (10 oz) English cucumbers

1 tablespoon sea salt

2 white part of green onions, julienne

Sauce

½ tablespoon red chilli flakes

2 teaspoons chilli paste *(gochu-jang)*

1 teaspoon rice vinegar

1 teaspoon sugar

½ teaspoon garlic, finely chopped

1 teaspoon green onion, chopped

Oi-saengchae

Method

오
이
생
채

1

Cut cucumbers in lengthwise and slice diagonally.

2

Sprinkle sea salt to cucumbers. Let it sit for 15-20 minutes.

3

Rinse a few times in cold water.
Squeeze out any excess water. Pat dry with paper towel.

When Koreans lose their appetite during the hot summer, this mouth-watering side dish is often served. With its refreshing subtle flavor, cucumber has endless serving and cooking possibilities. Due to its high water and almost zero calorie content, it is also one of the best weight controlling allies. The crunchy cucumber is mixed with a sweet, sour and spicy sauce. This simple summer dish surely refreshes your palate, mind, and body.

Tip

Oi-saengchae

4
Combine all ingredients for sauce along with the cucumbers.
Gently toss.

5
Garnish with green onion. Serve cold.

무
생
채

<u>03</u>
Mu-saengchae
Radish Salad

Serves 4 as an appetizer or as a side dish

Ingredients

500 g (1 lb) white radish, peeled

1 tablespoon sea salt

½ tablespoon red chilli flakes, finely ground

1 tablespoon rice vinegar

½ tablespoon sugar

1 teaspoon garlic, finely chopped

½ teaspoon ginger, finely chopped

Mu-saengchae

무
생
채

Method

1
Trim ends from radish. Julienne into 5 mm (¼ in). Place in a bowl.
Sprinkle salt onto radish. Mix well. Brine for 30 minutes.

2
Rinse several times in cold water. Drain. Squeeze any excess liquid.

Tip | *This simple salad goes well with meat or fish dishes.*
In order to enjoy its light, clean taste, slice the radish thinly. Serve it cold.

Mu-saengchae

3

Color radish with red chilli flakes.

4

Add rice vinegar, sugar, garlic, and ginger. Gently toss.

5

Serve cold or at room temperature.

콩
나
물
무
침

<u>04</u>

Kong-namul-muchim

Seasoned Bean Sprouts

Serves 4 as a side dish

Ingredients

250 g (9 oz) bean sprouts

6 cups water

1 tablespoon salt

½ teaspoon garlic, finely chopped

1 tablespoon green onion, sliced

1 tablespoon sesame oil

1 teaspoon sesame seeds

Kong-namul-muchim

Method

콩
나
물
무
침

1

Blanch bean sprouts for 30 seconds. Rinse in a cold water.
Drain and squeeze out any excess water.

Tip

Koreans love this humble, lightly cooked dish. To enjoy the crunchy texture of the bean sprouts, blanch the bean sprouts for a very short time in a boiling water.

Kong-namul-muchim

2

Season the bean sprouts with salt, garlic, green onion, sesame oil and sesame seeds.

3

Serve at room temperature.

도
토
리
묵
무
침

<u>05</u>

Dotori-muk-muchim

Acorn Jelly Salad

Serves 4 as a side dish or an entrée

Ingredients

450 g (16 oz) acorn jelly, cut into a bite size

½ cucumber, sliced

¼ onion, sliced

30 g (1 oz) Korean crown daisy,
cut into 3 cm (1 in) lengths

5 lettuce leaves, cut into a bite size

½ red chilli pepper, sliced

Sauce

Dressing

5 tablespoons soy sauce

2 tablespoons sesame oil

1 tablespoon sugar

2 tablespoons red chilli flakes

2 teaspoons green onion, chopped

1 teaspoon garlic, finely chopped

½ tablespoon sesame seeds, crushed

Dotori-muk-muchim

Method

도
토
리
묵
무
침

1
First, make the dressing. Combine all ingredients in a bowl.
Mix well.

2
Add acorn jelly and vegetables.
Gently toss with dressing.

Tip

Acorn jelly has no pronounced flavor of its own, but when it is tossed with a variety of vegetables and a sauce, it turns into a savory Korean style salad. This dish is refreshing, cool, and simple.

3
Garnish with red chilli pepper.
Serve cold or at room temperature.

Dotori-muk-muchim

버
섯
볶
음

<u>06</u>

Beoseot-bokkeum

Stir-fried Assorted Mushrooms

Serves 4 as a side dish

Ingredients

300 g (10 oz) assorted fresh mushrooms

30 g (1 oz) dried wood ear mushrooms, rehydrated

½ onion, julienne

½ tablespoon vegetable oil

Sauce

2 teaspoons soy sauce

¼ teaspoon salt

½ tablespoon sesame oil

2 tablespoons wild sesame seed powder

2 teaspoons water

Beoseot-bokkeum

Method

1

Mix all the ingredients for the sauce in a bowl. Set aside.

2

Trim the mushrooms. Tear mushrooms apart with hands.
Tear pieces similar in size.

버
섯
볶
음

Tip

Mushroom is an all-time favorite ingredient in Korean cuisine. It is eaten either fresh, poached, stir-fried, or pan-fried. In addition, added to a pancake mixture.
The seasoning sauce plays a major role in harmonizing the different flavour and textures of the mushrooms.

Beoseot-bokkeum

3

Heat vegetable oil in a pan. Stir-fry the onions and each mushroom
separately, over medium heat, with one pinch of salt.

4

Combine mushrooms with the sauce.
Cook for 3 minutes until the liquid has reduced.

5

Transfer to a plate. Serve immediately.

시
금
치
나
물

<u>07</u>

Sigeumchi-namul

Seasoned Spinach

Serves 4 as a side dish

Ingredients

250 g (9 oz) spinach

1 teaspoon salt

Sauce

2 teaspoons garlic, finely chopped

1 tablespoon green onion, chopped

½ tablespoon soy sauce

½ tablespoon sesame oil

1 teaspoon sesame seeds

Sigeumchi-namul

Method

1
Blanch spinach with salted water for 15 seconds.
Shock in cold water and drain. Squeeze out any excess liquid.

Tip

This salad is easy to make and delicious at room temperature. It is important to gather the freshest bunch of spinach, blanching it quickly in boiling water. The spinach will retain its vivid, green color and crunchy texture.

Sigeumchi-namul

2

Combine all the ingredients for the sauce with the spinach.
Gently toss.

3

Serve at room temperature.

호
박
나
물

<u>08</u>

Hobak-namul

Seasoned Zucchini

Serves 4 as a side dish

Ingredients

350 g (12 oz) zucchini

½ cup water

½ red chilli pepper, diagonally sliced

2 teaspoons salted shrimp (or fish sauce)

1 teaspoon garlic, finely chopped

1 tablespoon sesame oil

Hobak-namul

Method

호
박
나
물

1

Slice zucchini into half-moon-shapes and 0.5 cm (0.2 in) thickness.

2

Put the zucchini in a pot with ½ cup of water.

3

Par-cook the zucchini over low heat.

Tip

Many vegetable dishes appear easy to prepare. To make the dishes very delicious is quite tricky and require some skills. The secret is not to overcooked the vegetables. This enables the vegetables to retain the color, shape, and texture. This has to be one of the simplest recipes in Korean cuisine. It is easy and requires little time to make. The outcome is delicious!

Hobak-namul

4
Reduce heat to a gentle simmer.
Add salted shrimp and garlic to the pot.
Cook for 3 minutes.

5
Drizzle sesame oil and garnish with chilli pepper.

잡
채

<u>09</u>

Japchae

Stir-fried Glass Noodles and Vegetables

Serves 4 as an appetizer

Ingredients

2 dried *pyogo* (shiitake) mushrooms, rehydrated

4 dried wood ear mushrooms, rehydrated

100 g (3 ½ oz) oyster mushrooms, trimmed

150 g (5 oz) carrot, julienne

150 g (5 oz) onion, julienne

150 g (5 oz) spinach, trimmed

½ red chilli, julienne

100 g (5 oz) dried glass noodles, cooked or rehydrated

2 tablespoons vegetable oil

1 teaspoon salt

Egg pancakes, julienne

Sauce

6 tablespoons soy sauce

½ tablespoon sugar

1 teaspoon garlic, finely chopped

½ tablespoon green onion, chopped

1 tablespoon sesame oil

2 teaspoons sesame seeds, crushed

¼ teaspoon black pepper, ground

Japchae

Method

잡
채

1
Mix all ingredients for the sauce in a bowl.

2
Marinate the shiitake mushrooms with 1 teaspoon of the sauce.

3
Cut or tear apart the wood ear and oyster mushrooms with your
hands to make the pieces in similar thickness and length.

4
Heat 1 tablespoon of oil in a pan. Stir-fry the onions, carrots,
mushrooms and spinach separately, with a pinch of salt.
Set them aside in a large plate.

An absolute classic and all-time favorite Korean dish! Japchae used to be one of the royal dishes, and now it is served on special occasions for everyone to enjoy. Since the ingredients are selected based on five different colors, one can use whatever vegetables to make the dish vibrant. It can be served either hot or cold, making it an ideal dish either for buffets or potlucks.

Japchae

5
Heat 1 tablespoon of vegetable oil in a pan over medium-high heat.
Add the noodles, the vegetables and the sauce.
Stir-fry for 2 minutes. Cook until the noodles are clear.
If needed, add ⅓ cup of water.

6
Garnish with julienned egg pancakes.
Serve warm or at room temperature.

연
두
부

<u>10</u>
Yeondubu

Silken Tofu Salad

Serves 4 as an appetizer

Ingredients

300 g (10 oz) silken tofu

45 g (1 ½ oz) cup vegetable sprouts or baby greens

Sauce

Dressing

4 tablespoons soy sauce

1 tablespoon sesame oil

½ tablespoon sugar

1 tablespoon red chilli flakes

1 tablespoon sesame seeds, crushed

Yeondubu

Method

연
두
부

1

Mix all ingredients for the dressing in a bowl.

2

Place the tofu on the plate.

Tip

The unique, clean taste and creamy texture of tofu creates a fancy dance with a soy sauce based seasoning. Yeondubu is a tofu dish, which is usually served cold and lightly topped with a sauce. In this recipe, baby greens are included to enhance the texture. Since tofu has no pronounced flavor of its own, it complements well with a spicy dressing.

3
Pour dressing over tofu.
Add the vegetable sprouts on the top.
Serve immediately.

Yeondubu

두 부 조 림

<u>11</u>

Dubu-jorim

Braised Tofu in Soy Sauce

Serves 4 as a side dish

Ingredients

300 g (10 oz) firm tofu

½ cup corn starch

3 tablespoons vegetable oil

Sauce

1 teaspoon red chilli pepper, chopped

1 teaspoon green chilli pepper, chopped

1 teaspoon garlic, finely chopped

3 tablespoons soy sauce

2 teaspoons sesame oil

¼ cup water

3 tablespoons rice wine

1 tablespoon sugar

1 tablespoon red chilli flakes

Dubu-jorim

Method

두
부
조
림

1

Combine all the ingredients for the sauce in a bowl. Set aside.

2

Slice tofu into 1 cm (0.3 in) thickness and pat dry.
Lightly coat tofu pieces in corn starch.

3

Heat vegetable oil in a pan over medium heat.
Fry tofu until lightly browned and crisp.
Remove from oil and drain well.

Tip

In a traditional recipe, tofu is pan-fried and then it is simmered in a sauce.
In this recipe, however, the tofu is coated in a starch, fried, and then topped with a sauce.
The texture of the tofu becomes a crusty exterior, turning it into a very special side dish.

Dubujorim

4
Place sauce in the pan and bring to a boil.
Reduce the heat and simmer for about 2 minutes.
Slide tofu into pan and simmer until the sauce thickens.

5
Serve warm or at room temperature.

녹두빈대떡

<u>12</u>
Nokdu-bindae-tteok

Mung Bean Pancake

Serves 4 as an appetizer or an entrée

Ingredients

1 cup mung beans *(nokdu)*

1 tablespoon glutinous rice powder

150 g (5 oz) napa cabbage kimchi, chopped

1 tablespoon green onion, chopped

½ tablespoon onion, chopped

1 tablespoon sesame oil

⅓ teaspoon salt

¼ black pepper, ground

2 tablespoons vegetable oil

⅓ red and green chilli peppers, sliced

Sauce

Dipping sauce

2 tablespoons soy sauce

1 tablespoon vinegar

½ teaspoon red chilli flakes

Nokdu-bindae-tteok

Method

녹두빈대떡

1

Rinse the mung beans under running water.
Place in a bowl and cover with water. Soak for overnight until plump.

2

Discard soaking water and rub beans hard. Rinse under water to remove
the skins. Repeat several times until the beans have been peeled.

3

Put the beans into a blender.
Pour equal amount of water and blend.

4

Add glutinous rice powder and sesame oil.
Blend until it becomes a creamy consistency.

Tip

Nokdu-bindae-tteok is a classic savory mung bean pancake. It is served on traditional holidays and special occasions. There are many variations of this pancake, depending the region. This pancake will taste best when it's freshly made, dip in soy sauce and chillies. You can make delicious nokdu-bindae-tteok only with mung beans. However, by adding pork or kimchi you can enhance the flavor of this beloved pancake.

Nokdu-bindae-tteok

5

Combine ground mung beans with Kimchi and vegetables.
Season with salt and pepper.

6

Heat oil in a pan over medium heat.
Add one tablespoon of the mixture to the pan.

7

Cook until pancake is light golden.
Flip over and cook on the other side. Garnish with chillies on top.

8

Serve immediately with dipping sauce.

* You may buy beans that have already had the skins removed

비
빔
국
수

<u>13</u>

Bibim-guksu

Spicy Noodles

Serves 4 as a meal

Ingredients

450 g (16 oz) dried thin noodles

1 onion, julienne

200 g (7 oz) carrot, julienne

5 wild sesame leaves (perilla leaf), chiffonade

2 hard-boiled eggs, cut in half

200 g (7 oz) cabbage kimchi, chopped

1 tablespoon sesame oil

Sauce

3 tablespoons chilli paste *(gochu-jang)*

2 tablespoons red chilli flakes

4 tablespoons soy sauce

2 tablespoons sesame oil

3 tablespoons rice vinegar

3 tablespoons sugar

1 teaspoon garlic, finely chopped

1 tablespoon sesame seeds, crushed

Bibim-guksu

Method

비빔국수

1

To make the sauce, mix all the ingredients in a bowl.

2

Bring a pot of water to a boil. Add noodles and cook for 3 minutes.
Drain the noodles under cold water. Rinse two to three times.
Coat with 1 tablespoon of sesame oil.

Tip | *Bibim-guksu is made with thin, wheat-flour noodles called somyeon. The dish is easy to prepare and extremely tasty. It is especially popular during the summer months in Korea. Subtle and full of spiciness, it is a balanced of both sour and sweet. Bibim-guksu is a summer delicacy that brings back your lost appetite. It is a perfect summer time dish.*

Bibim-guksu

3

In a large mixing bowl, combine the noodles, onion, and carrots.
Add the sauce and mix well.

4

Place noodles in a bowl.
Garnish with kimchi and wild sesame leaves.
Top it off with a hard-boiled egg. Serve immediately.

콩국수

<u>14</u>

Kong-guksu

Noodles in Cold Soybean Soup

Serves 4 as a meal

Ingredients

2 cups soybeans

450 g (16 oz) thin noodles *(somyeon)*

10 cups water

¼ cucumber, julienne

1 teaspoon salt

Kong-guksu

Method

1
Soak soybeans in cold water overnight.
Rinse the soybeans in water several times. Boil for 20 minutes.

2
Rinse soybeans in cold water, removing the skin of the soybeans.

3
Blend soybeans with water until it becomes creamy.
Cover and store in the refrigerator.

Tip

Kong-guksu is a nutritious vegetarian food, packed with soy protein.
The key to making yummy soymilk for kongguksu is to properly cook the soybeans.

Kong-guksu

4
Cook noodles for 4-6 minutes.
Shock with cold water several times. Drain.

5
Place noodles in a bowl. Pour in the soybean broth.
Garnish with cucumber.

6
Serve it cold. Season with salt to taste.

감
자
수
제
비

<u>15</u>

Gamja-sujebi

Potato Hand-pulled Dough Flakes Soup

Serves 4 as a meal

Ingredients

100 g (3 ½ oz) potato, grated

1 cup all-purpose flour

1 ¼ cups cold water

1 teaspoon salt

1 ½ litres (1 ½ qts) anchovy stock

60 g (2 oz) zucchini, sliced

60 g (2 oz) potato, sliced

30 g (1 oz) green onion, sliced

1 ½ tablespoons light soy sauce

¼ teaspoon black pepper, ground

Gamja-sujebi

Method

감
자
수
제
비

1

Mix grated potato, all-purpose flour, and salt in a bowl.
To make the dough, gradually add water to the flour mixture.
Wrap the dough tightly in plastic.
Let the dough sit for 30 minutes at room temperature.

2

Bring stock to a boil in a large heavy-based pot.
Add zucchinis and potatoes.
Cook until the vegetables are par-cooked.

This dish is a good example of taking simple ingredients and transforming them to something special. Sujebi is a homemade dish that it is rarely served in restaurants. If you have a good quality homemade stock, this hand-pulled dough flakes soup would be a great dish to make at home.

Tip

Ganja-sujebi

3

Using your hands, roll the dough into a bite-sized pieces.
Put the dough pieces into a pot.
Cook until the dough floats to the surface.

4

Season with light soy sauce, black pepper, and salt.
Serve immediately.

순두부찌개

<u>16</u>
Sundubu-jjigae
Soft Tofu Stew

Serves 4 with steamed rice

Ingredients

600 g (1 lb 3 oz) soft tofu

1 litre (1 qt) water or anchovy stock

½ onion, sliced

200 g (7 oz) zucchini, sliced

1 tablespoon garlic, finely chopped

100 g (3 ½ oz) cabbage kimchi, chopped

4 tablespoons vegetable oil

1 ½ tablespoons red chilli flakes

300 g (10 oz) clams

1 tablespoon salted shrimp
(or 2 teaspoons fish sauce)

½ green onion, sliced

¼ red chilli pepper, sliced

¼ green chilli pepper, sliced

2 eggs (optional)

Method

순두부찌개

1

Heat the oil in a heavy-based pan.
Add the red chilli flakes over low heat. Keep stirring until the oil is
sizzling, taking careful not to burn the red chilli flakes.

2

Add onion, zucchini and kimchi.
Stir-fry for 2 minutes over low heat.

3

Add water or stock to the pot. Bring to a boil.

Tip

This dish is usually made with uncurdled tofu and vegetables. One can add mushrooms, onions and seafood. The dish is assembled and cooked directly in the serving vessel, which is traditionally made of thick, robust porcelain. The texture of this tofu stew is lovely and gentle. To make this dish, one needs the softest tofu that one can find. If you are vegetarian, you may substitute anchovy stock for vegetable stock and season with soy sauce or salt.

Sundubu-jjigae

4

Add clams. Scoop the soft tofu in big chunks. Bring to a boil.

5

Season with salted shrimp or fish sauce.

6

Add eggs. Keep cooking the eggs for about 30 seconds,
without stirring to make soft boiled or par-cooked eggs.

7

Garnish with chilli peppers and green onion. Serve immediately.

Seafood Dishes Packed with Iron and Mineral

Korean has four seasons; each season offers a different kind of seafood. With the appropriate knowledge about different seasonal seafood, you'll have a better chance to taste the delicacies of the sea at their best.

Seafood Dishes Packed with Iron and Mineral

Godeungeo-jorim
Braised Mackerel

Ojingeo-bokkeum
Stir-fried Squid

Myeolchi-bokkeun
Stir-fried Anchovies

Kkotge-tang
Spicy Blue Crab Stew

Miyeok-guk
Seaweed Soup

Haemul-pajeon
Seafood and Green Onion Pancake

고
등
어
조
림

<u>17</u>

Godeungeo-jorim

Braised Mackerel

Serves 4 with steamed rice

Ingredients

1 mackerel

2 cups anchovy stock

250 g (9 oz) white radish, sliced into 1.5 cm (0.5 in) thickness

100 g (3.5 oz) onion, sliced

½ stalk leek, sliced

Sauce

2 tablespoons soy sauce

1 ½ tablespoons red chilli flakes

1 tablespoon red chilli paste (gochu-jang)

1 tablespoon garlic, finely chopped

½ teaspoon ginger, finely chopped

2 tablespoons rice wine

1 tablespoon sugar

½ teaspoon black pepper, ground

Godeungeo-jorim

Method

고
등
어
조
림

1

Remove the head and fins from the mackerel.
Rinse, drain, and cut into 5 cm (2 in) lengths.

2

To make the sauce, combine all ingredients in a large bowl.
Mix well.

Tip

Mackerel is a rich source of DHA, so it's affectionately called "the barley of the sea." The seasoning sauce is made of soy sauce, red chilli paste, and red chilli flakes, which is a perfect match for this oily fish. This recipe also works well with Spanish mackerels or mackerel pike.

3

Place radish and onion on the bottom of a pot.
Add fish on top of the radish and onion.
Pour the sauce over the fish, adding 2 cups of anchovy stock.

4

Bring the pot to a boil. Reduce heat and simmer for about
20 minutes. Simmer until the radish and fish are fully cooked.

5

Garnish with leek. Serve immediately.

오
징
어
볶
음

<u>18</u>

Ojingeo-bokkeum

Stir-fried Squid

Serves 4 with steamed rice

Ingredients

2 squids

½ onion, sliced

½ green chilli pepper, sliced

½ red chilli pepper, sliced

1 tablespoon vegetable oil

3 tablespoons sea salt

Sauce

1 ½ tablespoons chilli paste *(gochu-jang)*

½ tablespoon red chilli flakes

1 tablespoon soy sauce

1 tablespoon rice wine

1 tablespoon sugar

1 tablespoon green onion, chopped

1 teaspoon garlic, finely chopped

½ teaspoon ginger, finely chopped

1 teaspoon sesame seeds, crushed

2 teaspoons sesame oil

¼ teaspoon salt

Ojingeo-bokkeum

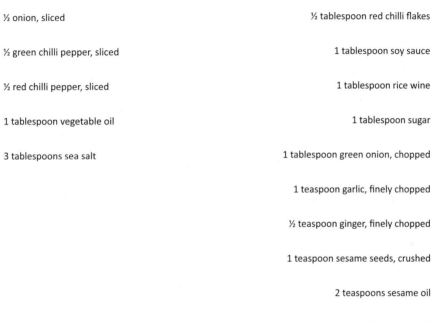

Method

▶ *Cleaning and scoring squid*

오
징
어
볶
음

1

Open body tube of squid. Remove skin by using sea salt.

2

Using a sharp knife, score shallow diagonal cuts in a crisscross
pattern on the inside surface.

3

Scoring squid makes it curl on contact with hot oil, while also al-
lowing flavors to penetrate into the squid.

4

Slice the scored squid in half and then into 4 cm (2 in) strips.

Tip

Squid and gochu-jang go very well together. It's a match with a spicy, hot, and happy ending. This dish is delicious and simple to prepare. Score shallow cuts on the surface of the squid so that the sauce can be absorbed. You can adjust the spiciness by adding more or less of the chilli flakes. The key is to cook the squid quickly over high heat. Otherwise, overcooking the squid results in a tough, chewy texture.

Ojingeo-bokkeum

1

Mix all ingredients for sauce in a bowl.

2

Heat a pan with vegetable oil over high heat.
Stir-fry the onions for 30 seconds. Add squid.
Stir-fry until the squid turns opaque.

3

Lower heat to a gentle simmer. Add sauce. Mix thoroughly.

4

Add chilli pepper. Stir-fry for 30 seconds.

멸
치
볶
음

<u>19</u>

Myeolchi-bokkeum

Stir-fried Anchovies

Serves 4-6 as a side dish

Ingredients

100 g (3 ½oz) small dried anchovies

3 tablespoons vegetable oil

3 tablespoons mixed nuts (optional), toasted and chopped

Sauce

2 teaspoons soy sauce

1 tablespoon sugar

3 tablespoons rice wine

3 tablespoons water

1 tablespoon honey

1 tablespoon sesame seeds

Myeolchi-bokkeum

Method

멸
치
볶
음

1
Roast dried anchovies in a heated pan for about 3 minutes.
Sieve in a strainer.

2
Stir-fry anchovies over medium high heat with oil for
about 3 minutes until they are crispy. Set aside.

3
Add all the ingredients for sauce to the pan. Bring to a boil.

Stir-fried anchovies are an all-time popular side dish in Korea. They are delicious as well as comforting. While larger anchovies are mostly used for making anchovy stock, smaller ones are often cooked with soy sauce or red chilli paste.

4
Lower the heat. Reduce the sauce until it thickens.
Add the anchovies and nuts to the pan. Quickly toss.

5
Arrange the anchovies on a small plate.
Garnish with sesame seeds. Serve at room temperature.

Myeolchi-bokkeum

113

꽃
게
탕

20

Kkotge-tang

Spicy Blue Crab Stew

Serves 4 with steamed rice

Ingredients

2 crabs, cleaned

250 g (9 oz) clams, cleaned

4 black tiger prawns, peeled and deveined

250 g (9 oz) white radish, sliced into 1.5 cm (0.5 in)

5 Korean water cress *(minari)*, cut into 4 cm (2 in)

5 crown daisy, cut into 4 cm (2 in)

½ green chilli pepper, sliced

½ red chilli pepper, sliced

½ green onion, sliced

4 cups anchovy stock

Sauce

Spicy paste

3 tablespoons soybean paste

3 tablespoons red chilli flakes

2 tablespoons soy sauce

½ tablespoon garlic, finely chopped

1 teaspoon ginger, finely chopped

3 tablespoons rice wine

¼ tablespoon black pepper, ground

Kkotge-tang

Method

꽃
게
탕

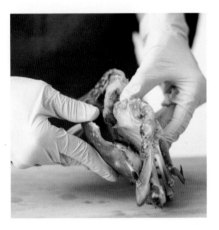

1

Combine all ingredients for the spicy paste. Set it aside.

2

Place the radish in a large heavy-based pot. Place seafood on top.

When the cold wind begins to blow, sea products, including crabs boast their best quality. This is the perfect time to make kkotge-tang. Spicy, hot kkotge-tang will taste a lot better when you share it with the people you love.

Kkotge-tang

3
Add the anchovy stock and spicy paste to the pot. Bring it to a boil.
Lower the heat and simmer for 10 to 15 minutes.

4
Garnish with Korean water cress, crown daisy, green onion
and chilli peppers. Serve immediately.

미
역
국

<u>21</u>

Miyeok-guk

Seaweed Soup

Serves 4 with steamed rice

Ingredients

60 g (2 oz) dried seaweed *(miyeock)*

300 g (10 oz) beef brisket, cut into a bite size

1 tablespoon garlic, finely chopped

3 tablespoons sesame oil

1 ½ litres (1 ½ qts) water

1 tablespoon light soy sauce

2 teaspoons salt

Miyeok-guk

Method

미역국

1
Soak dried seaweed in cold water for 30 minutes.

2
Rinse several times and drain. Cut into bite-sized pieces.

3
Heat sesame oil in a heavy-based pot.
Stir-fry the beef and seaweed with garlic for 3 minutes.

Tip

Seaweed is called super food. It is full of nutrients like calcium, potassium, and vitamins, and remains low in calories and fat. This soup is special. Koreans have the dish on their birthdays. It also has been served to women after giving a birth. It restores energy and good health. To make this soup, dried seaweed is rehydrated. Then cooked in a broth or plain water. One should keep in mind that when soaked, the dried seaweed expands and becomes almost ten times bigger in volume.

Miyeok-guk

4
Add water and bring to a boil.
Reduce the heat and simmer for 40 minutes.

5
Season with light soy sauce and salt. Serve immediately.

해
물
파
전

<u>22</u>

Haemul-pajeon

Seafood and Green Onion Pancake

Serves 4 as an appetizer or an entrée

Ingredients

10 small shrimps

½ squid, skinned

100 g (3 ½ oz) green onion

½ red and green chilli peppers,
diagonally sliced

2 eggs

2 tablespoons vegetable oil

Batter

1 cup all-purpose flour

⅔ cup ice-cold water

½ teaspoon salt

¼ teaspoon black pepper, ground

Sauce

Dipping Sauce

2 tablespoons soy sauce

1 tablespoon rice vinegar

½ teaspoon red chilli flakes

½ teaspoon sugar

Haemul-pajeon

Method

1

Trim the green onions. Cut in half if needed.
Beat the head of the green onions with backside of the knife.

2

Mix all of the ingredients for the batter in a bowl.
Add ice-cold water. Stir until the consistency becomes creamy.

3

Heat 2 tablespoons oil in a pan over medium heat. Pour ⅔ of the
batter into the pan and tilt the pan to cover the entire bottom.

Tip

This delicious pancake is crispy and colorful. The interior is moist and the exterior is crusty with lots of crunchiness. You can try this recipe using other ingredients like zucchini, kimchi with oysters. This versatile pancake is one of Koreans' favorite dish and easy to prepare.

Haemul-pajeon

4

Place green onions evenly on top of batter along with shrimps
and squid. Drizzle the rest of the batter on top.

5

Add the beaten eggs on top and garnish with chilli peppers.
Flip the egg mixture over. Cook on both sides.

6

Serve immediately with dipping sauce on the side.

Good Sources of Protein, Meat and Egg Dishes

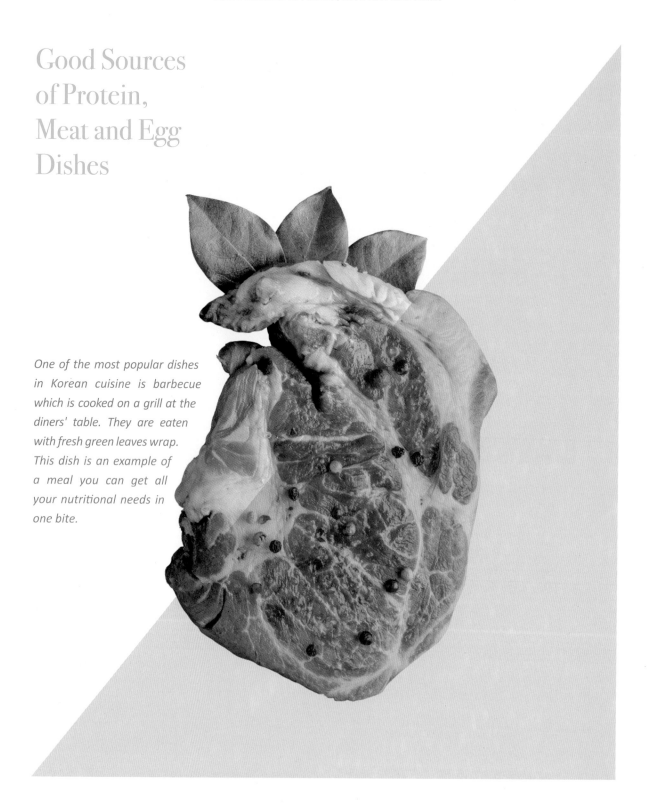

One of the most popular dishes in Korean cuisine is barbecue which is cooked on a grill at the diners' table. They are eaten with fresh green leaves wrap. This dish is an example of a meal you can get all your nutritional needs in one bite.

Good Sources of Protein, Meat and Egg Dishes

Bulgogi
Bulgogi

Galbi-gui
Grilled Beef Ribs

Galbi-jjim
Braised Short Ribs

Dak-galbi
Spicy Stir-fried Chicken

Dak-gangjeong
Fried Chicken with Flavored Soy Sauce

Jjim-dak
Braised Chicken in Soy Sauce

Samgyetang
Ginseng Chicken Soup

Bossam
Kimchi Wraps with Pork

Jaeyuk-bokkeum
Stir-fried Pork

Pyogobeoseot-jeon
Shiitake Mushroom Pancake

Gyeran-jjim
Steamed Eggs

Yukgaejang
Spicy Beef Soup

불
고
기

23

Bulgogi

Bulgogi

Serves 4 with steamed rice

Ingredients

600 g (1 lb 4 oz) beef sirloin or rib eye, thinly sliced

1 onion, julienne

120 g (4 oz) oyster mushrooms, trimmed

80 g (3 oz) Enoki mushrooms, trimmed

3 stalks green onion, sliced

2 tablespoons vegetable oil

Marinade

6 tablespoons soy sauce

1 tablespoon sugar

2 tablespoons sesame oil

1 tablespoon garlic, finely chopped

2 tablespoons green onion, chopped

150 g (5 oz) Korean pear, grated

½ tablespoon sesame seeds, crushed

½ teaspoon black pepper, ground

Bulgogi

Method

불
고
기

1

To marinate the beef, combine all the ingredients in a bowl.
Marinate the beef for at least 3 hours in the refrigerator.

2

Tear the mushrooms apart into equal size pieces.

3

Heat the oil in a pan over medium high heat.
Add the onions and sweat. Add the beef and gently stir-fry.

Tip

Preparation for a special meal on a special occasion usually begins with marinating the meat. Bulgogi is one of Korea's all-time favorite that is made with thinly sliced marinated beef. This is a classic Korean dish. The beef is bathed in soy sauce and then stir-fried. It is simple and easy to prepare as it is delicious. Beef can be an entrée on its own, but in this recipe the mushroom and the vegetables are added to maximize the flavor.

4
When beef is par-cooked, add the mushrooms to the pan.
Stir-fry until the liquid is reduced and then add the green onions.

5
Serve immediately.

갈비구이

24

Galbi-gui

Grilled Beef Ribs

Serves 4-6 with steamed rice

Ingredients

1 kg (2 lb) beef short ribs with bones
(about 4X5X6 cm or 1.5X2X4 in)

Marinade

5 tablespoons soy sauce

2 tablespoons rice wine

½ cup Korean pear, grated

1 ½ tablespoons sugar

1 tablespoon garlic, finely chopped

2 tablespoons green onion, chopped

1 teaspoon sesame seeds, crushed

2 tablespoons sesame oil

¼ teaspoon black pepper, ground

Galbi-gui

Method

갈비구이

1
Soak the beef ribs in cold water for 30 minutes to get rid of blood.
Drain and pat dry.

2
Use a sharp knife to trim any excess fat from beef ribs.

3
Slice meat through into 1.5 cm (0.5 in) thick,
leaving about 2.5 cm (1 in) from the end.

4
Fillet meat out from the bone into a thin strip.
Score both sides of the beef to tenderize the meat and to prevent
from curling when it is cooked under high heat.

In traditional Korean cuisine, beef is often cooked with soy sauce. Especially, beef ribs and soy sauce are a classic match. Before grilling the beef ribs, you should marinate it with a seasoning sauce. The longer the marinade, the better the flavoring. Beef ribs are versatile that you can cook it many different ways. It can be braised, grilled, or boil into a soup.

Tip

Galbi-gui

5
Roll the beef ribs, starting from the opposite side of bone to bone.

6
In a large bowl, combine all ingredients for the marinade with the beef ribs. Place the beef ribs in the refrigerator and marinade overnight. Ideally 12 to 24 hours.

7
Preheat a grill over medium-high heat.
Grill beef ribs and serve immediately.

갈비찜

<u>25</u>

Galbi-jjim

Braised Short Ribs

Serves 4-6 with steamed rice

Ingredients

1 kg (2 lb) beef short ribs with bones

200 g (7 oz) white radish, largely diced

150 g (5 oz) carrot, largely diced

1 onion, quartered

10 ginkgo nuts, peeled

2 dried *pyogo* (shiitake) mushrooms, rehydrated

4 chestnuts, peeled

6 dried jujubes

Marinade

⅓ cup soy sauce

1 cup water

2 tablespoons rice wine

1 ½ tablespoons sugar

3 tablespoons honey

½ cup Korean pear, grated

1 tablespoon garlic, finely chopped

1 tablespoon green onion, finely chopped

¼ teaspoon black pepper, ground

1 tablespoon sesame oil

Galbi-jjim

Method

갈
비
찜

1

Soak beef ribs in cold water for 2 hours to remove the blood.
Drain and pat dry.

2

Trim any excess fat from the beef ribs.

3

Blanch beef ribs in boing water for 3 minutes.
Shock them under cold water and then drain.

4

Combine beef ribs with the marinade in a large bowl.
Cover the large bowl and leave in the refrigerator for 2 hours to marinate.

Tip

Served at a royal table, galbi-jjim has been a traditionally special dish. Even today, it is one of the main dishes served on traditional holidays or special occasions. To enjoy the best quality of galbi-jjim, you should marinate the ribs to tenderize the meat. Special attention is paid to the time as well as to the preparation of dish.

Galbi-jjim

5
Dice the radish, carrot and onion into big pieces.
Remove seeds from dried jujubes. Cut the shiitake mushrooms in half.

6
Place marinated beef ribs in a large pot and bring to a boil.
Reduce the heat and simmer gently for 50 minutes.

7
Add radish, carrot, onion, ginkgo nuts, shiitake mushrooms,
chest nuts and jujubes. Cook for another 20 minutes.
Serve immediately.

닭
갈
비

<u>26</u>
Dak-galbi
Spicy Stir-fried Chicken

Serves 4 with steamed rice

Ingredients

1 whole chicken (450 g, 1 lb),
cut into big chunks

300 g (10 oz) cabbage, cut into big chuncks

100 g (3 ½ oz) sweet potato, thickly sliced

100 g (3 ½ oz) rice cakes (optional)

4 perilla leaves (wild sesame leaves), julienne

2 tablespoons vegetable oil

Marinade

1 teaspoon ginger, finely chopped

1 teaspoon garlic, finely chopped

1 tablespoon rice wine

1 tablespoon soy sauce

¼ teaspoon black pepper, ground

Sauce

3 tablespoons chilli paste *(gochu-jang)*

3 tablespoons soy sauce

2 tablespoons red chilli flakes (optional)

2 tablespoons rice wine

3 tablespoons rice syrup
(or 2 tablespoons honey)

1 tablespoon sesame oil

1 tablespoon garlic, finely chopped

1 tablespoon leek, finely chopped

2 teaspoons ginger, finely chopped

1 teaspoon salt

½ teaspoon black pepper

Dak-galbi

Method

닭
갈
비

1

Rinse the chicken well under cold water. Trim the any excess fat from
inside and outside cavity of the chicken. Marinade the chicken with
soy sauce, rice wine, garlic, ginger and black pepper for 20 minutes.

2

In a big bowl, combine all the ingredients for sauce with the chicken.
Mix well.

3

Heat the oil in a hot pot. Add the cabbages, sweet potatoes,
and the marinated chicken to the pan. Stir-fry for 1 minute.

Tip | *Dak-galbi is a delicious, spicy chicken dish. It is communal dish. Shared among a small, intimate group and a popular choice for friends. The dish stimulates conversation and naturally brings the group together for a fun night on the town. If you are not a big fan of spicy food, you can choose to take out the red chilli flakes.*

Dak-galbi

4

Add ½ cup of the water to the pan and stir fry for 10 minutes.

5

Add the rice cakes. Cook for an additional minute
or until the rice cakes are just tender.

6

Garnish with julienned perilla leaves. Serve immediately.

닭
강
정

<u>27</u>

Dak-gangjeong

Fried Chicken with Flavored Soy Sauce

Serves 4 as a snack

Ingredients

1 kg (2 lb) chicken thigh or breast,
cut into big chunks

1 cup milk

1 litre (1 qt) vegetable oil for frying

1 tablespoon green chilli pepper, chopped

1 tablespoon red chilli pepper, chopped

Frying Powder

30 g (1 oz) corn starch

70 g (2 oz) all-purpose flour

100 g (3 ½ oz) potato starch

30 g (1 oz) rice powder

1 teaspoon baking powder

Sauce

½ lemon, wedge

½ onion, diced

½ Korean pear, diced

½ apple, diced

1 tablespoon green chilli pepper, diced

1 tablespoon red chilli pepper, diced

3 cloves garlic, crushed

2 ginger, sliced

⅓ cup soy sauce

¾ cup water

3 tablespoons rice wine

1 tablespoon black peppercorns

1 bay leaf

5 tablespoons sugar

3 tablespoons honey

1 tablespoon vegetable oil

1 tablespoon sesame oil

Dak-gangjeong

Method

닭 강 정

1
Soak chicken in milk for 20 minutes. The milk help tenderizes the meat. Drain and pat dry with paper towel.

2
Combine all ingredients for the sauce in a pan. Bring to a boil and then reduce the heat. Simmer until the sauce thickens and is reduced in half. Turn off the heat. Set aside.

3
Gently toss chicken with frying powder. Set them aside.

4
Heat vegetable oil at the temperature of 160-170ºC (320-338ºF). Deep-fry the chicken until light-golden for 3 minutes. Remove and drain on paper towel.

Tip

There are a several different versions of this deep-fried chicken dish. This recipe is a soy sauce based. To give it an extra kick, add green and red chilli peppers.

Dak-gangjeong

5

Increase the vegetable oil to 180ºC (356ºF). Place the fried chicken
back into the oil. Deep-fry again until they are golden-brown.
Remove and drain on paper towel.

6

Reheat the sauce and add to the fried chicken.
Toss and mix thoroughly.

7

Garnish with green and red chilli peppers.
Serve warm or at room temperature.

찜
닭

<u>28</u>

Jjim-dak

Braised Chicken in Soy Sauce

Serves 4 with steamed rice

Ingredients

1 kg (2 lb) whole chicken, cut into big chunks

2 tablespoons vegetable oil

30 g (1 oz) dried glass noodle

200 g (7 oz) bok choy, trimmed

100 g (3 ½ oz) potato, largely diced

50 g (1 ½ oz) carrot, largely diced

60 g (1 ½ oz) onion, largely diced

2 dried red chillies

1 green onion, sliced

3 cloves garlic, sliced

Marinade

2 tablespoons rice wine

1 teaspoon salt

½ teaspoon black pepper, ground

⅓ teaspoon ginger, chopped

Sauce

2 cups water

5 tablespoons soy sauce

1 tablespoon rice wine

2 tablespoons honey

2 tablespoons sugar

2 teaspoons sesame oil

1 tablespoon garlic, finely chopped

1 teaspoon ginger, finely chopped

2 teaspoons sesame seeds, crushed

Jjim-dak

149

Method

1
To make the sauce, add all the ingredients in a large bowl. Set aside.

2
Rinse the chicken under cold water.
Trim away any excess fat from inside and outside of the cavity.
Marinate the chicken in a marinade for 20 minutes.

3
Heat oil in a heavy-based pot. Add garlic to make the garlic oil.

4
Add the marinated chicken.
Sauté over medium heat until the chicken is golden brown.

찜
닭

Tip

This dish is one of the most popular chicken dishes in Korea. It is often called Andong jjimdak, after the name of the city the dish originated from. Usually a whole chicken is cooked over high heat. Jjim-dak is braised in a sweet soy sauce seasoning. Add some dried chillies to give it an extra kick.

Jjim-dak

5

Add sauce, potatoes, carrots and onions to the pot. Bring to a boil.

6

Reduce the heat to a gentle simmer. Add the dried chillies.
Keep simmering with the lid on for about 30 minutes
until the vegetables are fully cooked.

7

Add the glass noodles. Cook for another 5 minutes.
Serve immediately.

삼
계
탕

<u>29</u>

Samgyetang

Ginseng Chicken Soup

Serves 4 as a meal

Ingredients

4 whole young chickens

1 tablespoon salt

½ tablespoon black pepper, ground

Stuffing

400 g (14 oz) glutinous rice

4 small fresh ginsengs

4 chestnuts

8 cloves garlic

4 dried jujubes

Stock

5 litres (5 qts) cold water

3 milk vetch roots (optional)

1 onion

30 g (1 oz) ginger, peeled

2 stalks leek

1 tablespoon black peppercorns

Samgyetang

Method

삼
계
탕

1
Wash glutinous rice and soak in cold water for 2 hours.
Drain and divide into four servings.

2
Put all the ingredients for stock in a big pot. Bring to a boil.
Lower the heat. Simmer for 40 minutes.

3
Remove internal organs and excess fat from chicken cavity.
Cut the head, tail, and end parts of the wings.

Tip

Ginseng chicken soup Samgyetang is a hot, steaming, delicious chicken soup. It is a small chicken stuffed with glutinous rice, ginseng, garlic and jujube. Samgyetang is a traditional Korean healthy food served to boost one's energy during the hot summer. Its savory broth with various spices and herbs, enriches the flavor and taste of the chicken. One whole small chicken is usually served per person.

Samgyetang

4
Stuff each chicken with 100g of rice, 1 ginseng, 1 chestnut,
2 cloves of garlic, and 2 dried jujubes.

5
Cross the chicken legs and tie with cooking thread.

6
Place the stuffed chicken into the stock. Bring to a boil. Lower the
heat. Simmer for 50 minutes until the chicken is fully cooked.
Transfer the chicken into a serving bowl. Pour the broth over the chicken.
Season with salt and pepper.

보
쌈

<u>30</u>

Bossam

Kimchi Wraps with Pork

Serves 4 with steamed rice

Ingredients

1 ½ kg (3 lb 3 oz) pork belly or shoulder

250 g (9 oz) cabbage kimchi, cut in a bite size

Stock

2 litres (2 qts) water

2 stalks leek

8 cloves garlic, crushed

1 tablespoon black peppercorns

5 cloves

3 bay leaves

6 dried jujubes

2 tablespoons soy bean paste

Bossam

보
쌈

Method

1
Put all stock ingredients into a pot and bring it to the boil.

2
Add pork and cook in a medium heat.
Turn down the heat to low and cook for another 10 minutes.

Tip

Bossam is a boiled pork dish, Ssam means "wrap" and Bossam means wrap with lots of generous stuffing inside. This is a tender pork dish served with fresh kimchi and wrapped in cabbage leaves. The pork is boiled and simmered with vegetables and spices to deepen the flavor. The thinly sliced pork, various toppings, and kimchi are wrapped in the napa cabbage kimchi leaves. It is a flavorful mixture of savory pork and spicy filling, which is guaranteed to please your taste buds.

Bossam

3

Take the cooked pork and let it cool down until ready to serve.

4

Slice the pork into 0.3 cm (0.2 in) thick pieces.

5

Put them on a large platter with kimchi at a side.

제
육
볶
음

31

Jaeyuk-bokkeum

Stir-fried Pork

Serves 4 with steamed rice

Ingredients

Sauce

600 g (1 lb 4 oz) pork belly or shoulder, sliced

4 tablespoons chilli paste *(gochu-jang)*

1 onion, sliced

2 tablespoons red chlilli flakes (optional)

1 tablespoon vegetable oil

4 tablespoons soy sauce

2 green onions, cut in 5 cm (2 in) lengths

2 tablespoons sugar

½ tablespoon sesame oil

½ tablespoon garlic, finely chopped

1 teaspoon ginger, finely chopped

Jaeyuk-bokkeum

Method

제
육
볶
음

1
First, make the sauce in a bowl.

2
Heat the vegetable oil in a pan over medium high heat.
Stir-fry the onions for 30 seconds.

3
Add pork and fully cook. Drain excess fat (oil) from pan.

Tip

Jaeyuk-bokkeum is a delicious Korean dish, which consists of marinated pork loin. It is stir-fried with red chilli pepper paste, gochu-jang. The chilli sauce is the base of the dish, which determines the flavor and its level of spiciness. Depending on one's taste, the spiciness can be softened by adding more soy sauce and less gochu-jang. This dish is a popular appetizer. One can eat and drink soju with it or serves as a great, hearty meal with rice and several side dishes.

4

Reduce the heat to a gentle simmer and add the sauce to the pan.
Combine the sauce with the pork and onion. Garnish with green onion.

5

Serve immediately.

Jaeyuk-bokkeum

표
고
버
섯
전

<u>32</u>

Pyogobeoseot-jeon

Shiitake Mushroom Pancake

Serves 4 as an appetizer

Ingredients

20 *pyogo* (shiitake) mushrooms

100 g (3 ½ oz) firm tofu

250 g (9 oz) beef round, ground

½ cup all-purpose flour

2 eggs

2 tablespoons vegetable oil

Marinade

3 teaspoons soy sauce

½ teaspoon sugar

1 teaspoon green onion, chopped

½ teaspoon garlic, finely chopped

2 teaspoons rice wine

¼ teaspoon black pepper, ground

1 teaspoon sesame oil

¼ teaspoon sesame seeds, crushed

Sauce

1 tablespoon soy sauce

½ tablespoon water

½ tablespoon rice vinegar

Pyogobeoseot-jeon

Method

표
고
버
섯
전

1

Separate stems from mushrooms. Chop stems finely.

2

Blanch mushroom caps for 30 seconds. Drain.

3

Mash tofu. Squeeze out any excess liquid using cheesecloth.

4

Combine stems, tofu, and beef marinade in a bowl.
Let it for 20 minutes.

Pyogobeoseot-jeon

Tip *Korean pancakes are traditionally served as a side dish while drinking. Jeon is made with many different ingredients like meat, vegetables, and seafood. The dish is best cooked slowly over low heat. Pyogo (Shiitake) mushroom is called the "meat of the forest" as a good source of nutrition.*

5

Dust the underside of mushroom caps with flour.
Stuff with marinated ingredients. Dust flour onto stuffed mushrooms.

6

Dip mushrooms into beaten eggs to lightly coat.

7

Pan-fry mushrooms over medium heat with 2 tablespoons
of vegetable oil. Pan-fry until golden-brown on both sides.

8

Make dipping sauce. Serve.

계
란
찜

<u>33</u>

Gyeran-jjim

Steamed Eggs

Serves 4 as a side dish

Ingredients

4 eggs

⅔ cup water

1 teaspoon salted shrimp (or fish sauce)

1 tablespoon green onion, chopped

¼ teaspoon red chilli flakes

Gyeran-jjim

Method

계
란
찜

1

Add water in a small thick bottom pot and bring to a boil.

2

Beat eggs, salted shrimp, and salt in bowl until well blended.

3

Pour in egg mixture to the pot and lower the heat to a minimum.
Keep stirring the egg mixture until it has almost thickened.

Tip

Gyeran-jjim is a very special dish that is shaped like a volcanic eruption. The main ingredients include eggs and water with optional ingredients such as green onions, red chilli flakes, salted shrimp sauce, pollack roe, and salt pepper. The dish is made by slowly heating the beaten eggs in a traditional earthenware pot or in a small thick bottom pot. Then quickly put the lid on when the mixture begins to rise. Compared to its simple recipe, one can master this dish with lots of practice and skill.

Gyeran-jjim

4

Cover the pot with a lid and cook for 7 minutes over low heat.

5

Garnish with green onion and red chilli flakes. Serve immediately.

* salted shrimp can be substitute to fish sauce or salt

육
개
장

34

Yukgaejang

Spicy Beef Soup

Serves 4 with steamed rice

Ingredients

600 g (1 lb 4 oz) beef brisket

2 litres (2 qts) water

150 g (5 oz) fiddle heads, 7 cm (3 in) lengths

150 g (5 oz) mung bean sprouts

3 stalks leek, cut in half lengthwise,
7 cm (3 in) lengths

2 tablespoons vegetable oil

Sauce

Seasoning

3 tablespoons soy sauce

3 tablespoons red chilli flakes

1 teaspoon salt

1 tablespoon sesame oil

1 tablespoon garlic, finely chopped

2 tablespoons green onion, chopped

¼ teaspoon black pepper, ground

Yukgaejang

Method

1

Place the beef in a large heavy-based pot with water. Bring to a boil.
Lower the heat. Simmer for 50 minutes until the meat becomes
tender. Skim the surface to remove any impurities.
Reserve the stock and beef separately.

2

Cut or tear the beef into bite-sized pieces.

3

Mix all the ingredients for the seasoning in a big bowl.

4

Blanch the fiddle heads and the mung bean sprouts separately
for 1 minute and then drain.

육
개
장

Tip

Yukgaejang is a highly nutritious dish, packed with beef and vegetables. The soup is smoky, spicy, and rich. It has healthy hunks of meat and plenty of vegetables that are soft but not mushy. A critical step is to blanch the vegetables before seasoning. You can also prepare dakgaejang, using chicken instead of beef. The soup is served with rice. It is delicious as well as satisfying, a very heartwarming soup.

Yukgaejang

5

Blanch the leek for 30 seconds and then drain.

6

Place all vegetables and beef in a pot. Gently toss with the seasoning.

7

Heat 1 tablespoon of oil in a pot. Stir-fry the seasoned vegetables and beef over medium heat for 3 minutes. Add the reserved stock and bring to a boil. Lower the heat to a gentle simmer. Cook for 50 minutes. Serve hot.

Gluten-free,
Rice and Rice Dishes

Korean has been cultivating grains and rice for many of centuries. Each meal is reflected around rice, grains and beans. Bread is almost never eaten during a meal. Koreans have regarded the first full moon day of the year as an important day and rice the guest of honor on this special day. People cooked five-grain rice and shared it with neighbors in hopes of peace and a good harvest.

Gluten-free,
Rice and Rice Dishes

Ssal-bap
Cooked White Rice

Chaeso-gimbap
Vegetable Gimbap

Bibimbap
Bibimbap

Kimchi-bokkeum-bap
Kimchi Fried Rice

Hobak-juk
Pumpkin Porridge

Tteokguk
Sliced Rice Cake Soup

Tteok-bokki
Stir-fried Rice Cake

쌀
밥

35

Ssal-bap

Cooked White Rice

Serves 4 (makes about 4 cups of cooked rice) as a meal

Ingredients

1 ½ cups short-grain rice

2 ⅔ cups water

Ssal-bap

Method

쌀
밥

1
Put rice in a sieve. Rinse well under running water and drain.
Soak rice in water for 1 hour and drain.

2
Put rice and water in a heavy-based pot. Bring to a boil.

Tip

When greeting each other, Koreans often ask "Have you eaten a meal?" A meal in this question implies rice. Traditionally Koreans eat steamed white short grain rice with almost every meal. This recipe makes fluffy, fully cooked rice!

Ssal-bap

3

Reduce the heat to gentle simmer. Cover the pot with a tight-fitting lid.
Cook for 10 minutes. Turn off the heat.
Let the rice sit for 10 minutes. Do not remove lid until it is finished.

4

Remove the pot from the stove.
Before serving, fluff the rice with a spoon.

채
소
김
밥

<u>36</u>

Chaeso-gimbap

Vegetable Gimbap

Serves 4 as a meal

Ingredients

4 cups steamed rice

4 dried *pyogo* (shiitake) mushrooms, rehydrated, julienne

200 g (7 oz) carrot, julienne

200 g (7 oz) spinach, trimmed

2 eggs

4 sheets toasted laver *(gim)*

2 tablespoons vegetable oil

2 tablespoons soy sauce

2 teaspoons salt

½ teaspoon black pepper

2 tablespoons sesame oil

2 teaspoons sesame seeds

Marinade

Marinade for *pyogo* (shiitake) mushrooms

2 teaspoons soy sauce

½ teaspoon sugar

1 teaspoon sesame oil

Chaeso-gimbap

Method

채
소
김
밥

1
Marinate shiitake mushrooms in marinade for 20 minutes.

2
Heat pan with 1 tablespoon of vegetable oil over medium high heat.
Stir-fry carrots and season with a pinch of salt and black pepper.

3
Blanch spinach for 10 seconds and rinse in cold water. Squeeze out excess
liquid and season with 1 teaspoon of soy sauce and 1 teaspoon of sesame oil.

4
Beat eggs in a bowl and season with a pinch of salt and pepper. Heat oil
in a pan with 1 teaspoon of vegetable oil over low heat and pour eggs.
Spread thinly and cook both sides. After cooling slice thinly.

5
Stir-fry shiitake mushrooms with 1 teaspoon of vegetable oil.

Tip

Gimbap is a Korean dish made with steamed white rice (bap) and various other ingredients, rolled in gim (sheets of toasted laver) and served in bite-size pieces. Gimbap is often eaten during picnics or outdoor events, or as a light lunch, served with danmuji or kimchi. Just like sandwiches, gimbap is easy to transport. One can have it any time and any place. You can also make a variety of gimbap, depending on the ingredients that you have available.

How to make rice rolls

1
Place steamed rice in a bowl. Mix in 1 tablespoon of sesame oil, ½ teaspoon of salt and 1 teaspoon of sesame seeds.

2
Place the shiny side of the toasted laver down on a bamboo rolling mat. Evenly spread 1 cup of rice over the toasted laver sheet, leaving about 5 cm (2 in) room on one side of the sheet.

3
Place mushrooms, carrot, eggs and spinach in the center of the rice.

4
Use both hands to tightly roll the mat. Brush finished roll with sesame oil. The sesame oil will give flavor and keep the gimbap shiny.

5
Cut into bite sized pieces and arrange on a platter. Serve at room temperature.

비
빔
밥

37

Bibimbap

Bibimbap

Serves 4 as a meal

Ingredients

4 cups steamed rice

200 g (7 oz) beef, julienne

150 g (5 oz) dried fiddle heads (gosari), rehydrated

150 g (5 oz) bean sprouts

150 g (5 oz) spinach, 5 cm (2 in) lengths

150 g (5 oz) carrot, julienne

4 sunny-side-up eggs

4 tablespoons chilli paste (gochu-jang)

1 tablespoon salt

3 tablespoons vegetable oil

Seasoning for carrots

1 teaspoon salt

¼ teaspoon black pepper, ground

Marinade

Marinade for beef

1 tablespoon soy sauce

1 teaspoon sugar

1 teaspoon garlic, finely chopped

1 teaspoon green onion, chopped

½ teaspoon sesame seeds, crushed

1 teaspoon sesame oil

½ teaspoon black pepper, ground

Marinade for fiddle heads

1 teaspoon soy sauce

½ teaspoon garlic, finely chopped

½ teaspoon green onion, chopped

2 teaspoons sesame oil

Bibimbap

Sauce

Sauce for blanched bean sprouts

1 teaspoon salt

1 tablespoon sesame oil

Sauce for blanched spinach

1 teaspoon soy sauce

1 tablespoon sesame oil

Method

1

Combine all the ingredients for the beef marinade in a bowl.
Marinate the beef for 30 minutes.

2

Combine all the ingredients for the fiddle heads marinade
in a bowl. Let it sit for 15 minutes.

3

Bring 5 cups of water to a boil and add ½ tablespoon of salt.
Blanch the bean sprouts for 30 seconds and shock them under cold
water. Drain off any excess water and season with the sauce.

4

Blanch spinach in the same pot of boiling water for 20 seconds and
shock them under cold water. Squeeze out any excess water and
season with the sauce.

비
빔
밥

Tip

The word bibimbap literally means "mixed rice". It is one of Korea's signature dish and a local favorite. Another variation is dolsot bibimbap, which is served in a hot stone bowl. One can enjoy the crusty rice at the bottom of the stone bowl along with the cooked meat and vegetables on top.

Bibimbap

5
Put 1 teaspoon of the vegetable oil in a pan and quickly stir-fry the carrots and season. Transfer to a plate.

6
In the same pan, stir-fry the beef and the fidde heads separately with 1 teaspoon of vegetable oil. Transfer to a plate.

7
Divide rice among four bowls.
Top with carrots, fiddle heads, bean sprouts, spinach, and beef.

8
Place a sunny-side-up egg on the center.
Serve the Bibimbap with chilli paste alongside.

김
치
볶
음
밥

<u>38</u>

Kimchi-bokkeum-bap

Kimchi Fried Rice

Serves 4 as a meal

Ingredients

450 g (15 oz) cabbage kimchi, chopped

200 g (7 oz) pork shoulder or belly, diced

½ onion, chopped

4 cups steamed rice

½ tablespoon sugar

1 tablespoon sesame oil

2 tablespoons vegetable oil

Garnish

½ cup green onion, chopped

4 eggs, sunny-side-up (optional)

Kimchi-bokkeum-bap

Method

김
치
볶
음
밥

1

Heat oil in a pan. Add pork and onion to the pan.
Stir-fry for 2 minutes until the pork is cooked and the onions have sweated.
Add kimchi and sugar. Stir-fry for 3 minutes.

If you have kimchi that has made about two weeks ago, it is strongly recommended that you make this dish. Anyone can make this very simple dish. It includes several ingredients, in addition to well-fermented kimchi.

Tip

2
Add rice. Stir-fry for another 3 minutes. Drizzle sesame oil to the rice.

3
Garnish with green onion and an egg. Serve immediately.

호
박
죽

<u>39</u>

Hobak-juk

Pumpkin Porridge

Serves 4 as a starter

Ingredients

500-600 g (1-1 ⅓lb) kabocha squash

½ cup glutinous rice powder

3 cups water

2 tablespoons sugar

1 teaspoon salt

Method

호
박
죽

1

Quarter the kabocha squash and remove the seeds.

2

Steam the kabocha squash for 20 minutes until it is fully cooked.

3

Peel the skin off and dice roughly.

4

Blend the kabocha squash with 3 cups of water to make the puree.
Add rice powder and keep blending.
Add water to control the thick, creamy consistency.

Tip | *As it is easy to digest, pumpkin porridge is often served for breakfast, as a light meal, or as baby food in Korea. The recipe is quite simple. The pumpkin is peeled, cubed, boiled. Then glutinous rice power is added to thicken the porridge. As easy as it is to prepare, this soup still requires attention and time.*

Hobak-juk

5

Transfer the puree into a heavy-based pot. Bring to a boil.
Lower the heat to a gentle simmer. Cook for 20 minutes until the
kabocha squash is cooked and becomes a creamy consistency.

6

Garnish with pumpkin seed. Serve immediately.
Season with sugar and salt to your liking.

떡국

<u>40</u>

Tteokguk

Sliced Rice Cake Soup

Serves 4 as a meal

Ingredients

450 g (16 oz) rice cake, thinly sliced

1 egg

1 ½ litres (1 ½ qts) beef stock

2 tablespoons light soy sauce

½ teaspoon salt

¼ teaspoon black pepper, ground

Tteokguk

199

Method

떡
국

1
Rinse and soak the rice cakes in cold water for 20 minutes.

2
Separate the egg yolk from the egg white. Beat separately.
To make the egg garnish, heat a lightly-oiled pan.
Pan fry the egg yolk and egg white separately. Set aside.
Cut the egg pancakes into a diamond shape.

Tip

The rice cake used to make tteokguk is formed into a long cylinder shaped, called "garaetteok."
Its shape is symbolic, wishing for longevity in life. The oval shape of the rice cakes resembles
coins, another symbol for wealth and prosperity. When people are eating tteokguk, they are
praying for a good year and adding one more year to their age. Koreans eat tteokguk as their
first meal on Lunar New Year's Day. This traditional dish is believed to bring a happy new year.

Tteokguk

3
Bring stock to a boil in a large heavy-based pot. Add the rice cakes.
Cook for about 10 minutes, until softened.
Season with light soy sauce, salt, and black pepper.

4
Garnish with the egg pancakes. Serve immediately.

떡
볶
이

<u>41</u>

Tteok-bokki

Stir-fried Rice Cake

Serves 4 as an entrée or as a snack

Ingredients

450 g (16 oz) rice cakes

200 g (7 oz) fish cakes, cut into a bite size

2 cups anchovy stock or water

½ green onion, thinly sliced

2 hard-boiled eggs (optional)

Sauce

3 tablespoons chilli paste *(gochu-jang)*

1 tablespoon sugar

1 tablespoon soy sauce

1 tablespoon red chilli flakes (optional)

2 teaspoons garlic, finely chopped

2 teaspoons sesame oil

Tteok-bokki

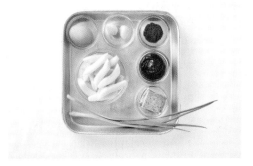

Method

1
First, make the sauce. Put all ingredients in a bowl. Mix well.
Let it stand for 15 minutes.

2
Bring stock (or water) to a boil in a large heavy-based pan.

3
Lower the heat. Add the fish cakes and sauce.
Cook for about 3 minutes.

Tip

Tteok-bokki is a beloved Korean dish, with many variations and a rich history. Literally translated as "stir-fried rice cake." Tteok-bokki is made with garaetteok, a cylinder-shaped, white rice cake. Tteok-bokki is one of the most popular Korean snacks. A memorable dish in for many of Korea students' school days. The mixture of red chilli paste, green onion, garlic, and red chilli flakes makes it tasty, sweet, and spicy tteok-bokki.

Tteok-bokki

4
Add the rice cakes.
Cook until the rice cakes are soften and the sauce has thickened.

5
Carefully placed the peeled eggs in the sauce. Turn off the heat.
Cut the eggs in half and arrange on a platter.
Spoon the sauce mixture over the platter. Garnish with green onion.
Serve immediately.

A Gold Mine of Vitamins, Kimchi and Fermented Foods

Kimchi is a classic Korean vegetable side dish which is considered a nutritional powerhouse. It is low in calories and packed with vitamins, minerals, and fiber which can help fill you up without filling you out. Fermented food aids digestions and it is full of beneficial enzymes that help us stay in optimal health.

A Gold Mine
of Vitamins,
Kimchi and
Fermented Foods

Baechu-kimchi
Kimchi

Oi-sobagi
Cucumber Kimchi

Kkakdugi
Diced Radish Kimchi

Geot-jeori
Fresh Kimchi (Korean Salad)

Kimchi-jeon
Kimchi Pancake

Dubu Kimchi
Stir-fried Kimchi with Tofu

Kimchi-jjigae
Kimchi Stew

Doenjang-jjigae
Soybean Paste Stew

배
추
김
치

<u>42</u>

Baechu-kimchi

Kimchi

Serves 4-6 with steamed rice

Ingredients

1 napa cabbage (about 3 kg or 6-7 lb)

Brine

250 g (8 oz) sea salt

2 litres (2 qts) water

Sauce

Seasoning Mixture

400 g (14 oz) white radish,
julienne into 0.5 cm (0.2 in) thickness

100 g (3 ½ oz) green onion,
cut into 4 cm (2 in) lengths

½ cup red chilli flakes

3 tablespoons salted shrimp
(or ⅓ cup fish sauce)

2 tablespoons sugar

1 tablespoon garlic, finely chopped

2 teaspoons ginger, finely chopped

Method

1

Remove the discolored outside leaves of the cabbages and trim stem. Cut the cabbage lengthwise into half.

2

In a big bowl, add salt to the water. Brine cabbage overnight until the cabbage leaves are flexible.

3

Rinse several times in cold water. Drain enough for about 30 minutes to remove any excess liquid from the cabbage.

4

Combine red chilli flakes, garlic, ginger, salted shrimp and sugar with radish. Toss well. Add green onion to the mixture. Gently toss.

배추김치

Tip

Kimchi is a must item at every Korean table. There are more than 100 kinds of kimchi, but napa cabbage kimchi is the most popular kind. While chilli peppers are the predominant spice and often the most visible ingredient, other items such as salted shrimp, garlic, green onions and ginger play an important role, not only for flavor, but also in the fermentation process.

Baechu-kimchi

5

Place cabbage on a tray and stuff inside leaves with the seasoning mixture. Smear leaves generously on both sides with the seasoning mixture.

6

Tightly press the leaves together. Wrap the center with the outer leaf to make a bundle. Prepare the rest of cabbage in the same manner.

7

Transfer cabbages into a container and keep at room temperature for half a day.

8

Afterwards, store in the refrigerator. If you want to try well-fermented kimchi, let it sit longer in the refrigerator and eat after 2 or 3 days.

오
이
소
박
이

<u>43</u>

Oi-sobagi

Cucumber Kimchi

Serves 6 as a side dish

Ingredients

1 kg (2 lb) cucumbers (about 4 large English,
5 Persian, 8 Kirby cucumbers)

60 g (2 oz) Korean chive, chopped

60 g onion, chopped

Brine

100 g (3 ½ oz) sea salt

1 litre (1 qt) water

Sauce

Stuffing

3 tablespoons red chilli flakes

3 tablespoons soy sauce

2 teaspoons garlic, finely chopped

1 teaspoon ginger, finely chopped

1 teaspoon sugar

1 teaspoon salt

Oi-sobagi

Method

1

Cut cucumbers into 7.5 cm (3 in) lengths and cut them in
lengthwise into quarters, leaving about 2.5 cm (1 inch) at the base uncut.

2

Brine cucumbers in salted water for about 40 minutes
until flexible. Rinse several times. Drain. Squeeze away any excess liquid.

Tip *Cucumber kimchi is made by turning a cucumber into a pocket, adding it with vegetables and kimchi paste. Mostly made in summer when cucumber is in season. Cucumber kimchi is a prime example of a kimchi that does not have to be fermented. Just give it one or two days, it is ready to be served on your table to enjoy. All you have to do is to brine the cucumber to enhance the crunchy texture. Rinse it in cold water and season.*

Oi-sobagi

3
Mix all ingredients for the seasoning in a bowl.
Add cucumbers to the seasoning mixture.

4
Transfer to a container. Store in the refrigerator for 1 day. Serve.

깍두기

44

Kkakdugi

Diced Radish Kimchi

Serves 4-6 as a side dish

Ingredients

450 g (15 oz) white radish, medium diced

½ cup green onion,
cut into 4 cm (1.5 in) lengths

⅓ cup Korean water cress *(minari)*,
cut into 4 cm (1.5 in) lengths

2 tablespoons red chilli flakes

1 tablespoon fish sauce

½ tablespoon garlic, finely chopped

2 teaspoons ginger, finely chopped

1 tablespoon sugar

Sauce

Brine

1 litre (1 qt) hot water

⅔ cup salt

Kkakdugi

깍
두
기

Method

1

Brine the radish in salted hot water. Let it sit for 20 minutes.

2

Drain the radish. Rinse several times.

3

Color the radish with red chilli flakes.

4

Add fish sauce, garlic, ginger, and sugar. Toss well.

Tip

Kkakdugi is a popular side dish, eaten with a Korean soup. As it is eaten before over-fermentation, ideally to be consume within ten days. Radish produced in the fall has a crisp, crunchy texture, which makes kkakdugi extremely delicious.

Kkakdugi

5
Add green onion and Korean water cress. Mix thoroughly.

6
Place the radish kimchi in a container.
Leave the container at room temperature in a cool place for a half day.
Then put in the refrigerator. Serve the next day.

겉
절
이

<u>45</u>

Geot-jeori

Fresh Kimchi (Korean Salad)

Serves 4 as a side dish or an entrée

Ingredients

250 g (9 oz) mixed leafy greens

45 g (1 ½ oz) Korean chives
(or green onion), cut into 2.5 cm (1 in)

120 g (4 oz) apple, thinly sliced

45 g (1 ½ oz) onion, thinly sliced

Sauce

Dressing

3 tablespoons soy sauce

2 tablespoons rice vinegar

1 tablespoon sugar

1 tablespoon red chilli flakes

1 tablespoon sesame seeds, crushed

1 teaspoon garlic, finely chopped

1 teaspoon green onion, chopped

Geot-jeori

Method

걸
절
이

1
First, make the dressing. Combine all ingredients in a bowl. Mix well.

2
Tear leafy greens into a bite-sized pieces.
Slice the onion and rinse in cold water. Drain.

Tip *If you do not have any kimchi at home and craving a fresh vegetable dish, try making this salad. It is simple to prepare. One can simply use any leafy green vegetables in the refrigerator to make a geot-jeori salad. Prepare the greens and then add the seasoning mix to the vegetables. Gently toss the salad. It is best if you have a variety of colorful vegetables with different textures. Geot-Jeori is a wonderful, tasty Korean-style salad.*

3

Combine the reserved vegetables in a large bowl
and mix with the dressing. Toss well. Serve immediately.

Geot-jeori

김
치
전

<u>46</u>

Kimchi-jeon

Kimchi Pancake

Serves 4 as an appetizer

Ingredients

1 cup cabbage kimchi, chopped

2 cups all-purpose flour

1 ½ cups ice-cold water

¼ teaspoon salt

¼ teaspoon black pepper, ground

2 tablespoons vegetable oil

Sauce

Dipping sauce

2 tablespoons soy sauce

1 tablespoon vinegar

1 teaspoon sugar

Kimchi-jeon

Method

김
치
전

1

Add salt and pepper to all-purpose flour. Make batter by adding
ice-cold water until it becomes a creamy consistency.

2

Add kimchi to the batter and stir.

3

Heat the vegetable oil in a pan. Pour batter and spread.
Cook the pancake until the bottom becomes crispy,
golden-brown.

Tip

Kimchi by itself is a good side dish. For its versatility, it can be transformed to make a new dish like kimchi-jeon. In Korea, kimchi-jeon is a popular choice, adored by everyone.

Kimchi-jeon

4

Turn it over and thoroughly cook the pancake.
Transfer the pancake to a plate.

5

In a bowl, mix all ingredients for the dipping sauce.

6

Serve immediately with dipping sauce on the side.

두
부
김
치

<u>47</u>

Dubu Kimchi

Stir-fried Kimchi with Tofu

Serves 4 as an appetizer or an entrée

Ingredients

300 g (10 oz) firm tofu

300 g (10 oz) napa cabbage kimchi,
cut into a bite size

¼ medium-sized onion, sliced

1 tablespoon garlic, finely chopped

1 teaspoon sugar

2 tablespoons sesame oil

2 tablespoons vegetable oil

½ tablespoon salt

1 teaspoon black sesame seeds

Dubu Kimchi

Method

두부김치

1
Heat vegetable oil in a pan over medium high heat.
Add onion, kimchi, and garlic. Stir-fry for 3 to 5 minutes.
Finish by adding sesame oil.

2
Poach tofu in hot water for 3 minutes. Drain.
Slice the tofu into thick slices.

Tip

Dubu kimchi is Korean's favorite "ahn-joo" (food that complements alcoholic beverages). Therefore, this makes dubu kimchi a great party food. However, it can also be enjoyed as an entrée or snack any time of the day. The incredibly, flavorful, mix of kimchi and seasoned pork is well balanced with the wholesomeness of the tofu. It can also be a great vegetarian dish, by omitting the pork. You can serve dubu kimchi alone or with steamed rice. It goes well with soju (vodka-like Korean drink) and makgeolli (milky rice wine).

Dubu Kimchi

3

Arrange the tofu slices with the stir-fried kimchi on a platter.
Garnish with black sesame seeds. Serve immediately.

김
치
찌
개

<u>48</u>
Kimchi-jjigae
Kimchi Stew

Serves 4 with steamed rice

Ingredients

450 g (15 oz) cabbage kimchi, chopped

100 g (3 ½ oz) pork, diced

50 g (1 ½ oz) onion, sliced

1 teaspoon garlic, finely chopped

2 teaspoons sugar

1 teaspoon soy sauce

4 cups vegetable stock

1 green onion, sliced

1 tablespoon vegetable oil

Kimchi-jjigae

Method

김
치
찌
개

1
Heat vegetable oil in a large heavy-based pot.
Stir-fry the pork and kimchi for about 3 minutes.

2
Add onion, garlic, sugar and soy sauce to the pot.

Tip

If you like kimchi, you should try this delicious stew. You will taste the different flavor from the fresh kimchi. Adding other ingredients like pork, onion, and leek will enhance the flavor of the stew.

Kimchi-jjigae

3
Pour stock to the pot. Bring to a boil.
Reduce heat and simmer for 20 minutes.

4
Garnish with green onion. Serve immediately.

된
장
찌
개

<u>49</u>

Doenjang-jjigae

Soybean Paste Stew

Serves 4 with steamed rice

Ingredients

6 cups vegetable stock

5 tablespoons soybean paste *(doen-jang)*

100 g (3.5 oz) potato, diced

100 g (3.5 oz) firm tofu, diced

100 g (3.5 oz) zucchini, sliced

60 g (2 oz) oyster mushrooms thinly cut

½ green onion, sliced

½ red and green chilli peppers, sliced

Doenjang-jjigae

Method

1
Cut vegetables and tofu into bite size.

2
Bring stock to a boil in a heavy-based pot.
Add potatoes and cook until they are tender but not falling apart.

된
장
찌
개

Tip

Once you have prepared all the ingredients, this stew is more than half way done. The secret to making this stew is adding the ingredients at different stages. You will notice that the vegetables and soybean paste are added first and the tofu and mushroom are added last because of these ingredients take less time to cook. This will result in a myriad of flavor and vivid textures.

3

Add soybean paste, zucchini and stir to combine the ingredients.
Cook on high heat for about 10 minutes. Lower the heat and add
tofu and oyster mushrooms. Simmer for another 5 minutes.
Check seasoning to your liking.

4

Garnish with red, green chillies and green onion.
Serve hot immediately.

Doenjang-jjigae

Nutritious Snacks and Desserts That Boost Your Happiness

Desserts leave your palate clean and you feel refreshed. These foods fill you up for longer instead of pulling you down like with salt, butter and sugar.

Nutritious Snacks and Desserts That Boost Your Happiness

Sujeonggwa
Cinnamon Punch

Patbingsu
Korean Shaved Ice with Sweet Red Bean

Hotteok
Pan-fried Sweet Pancake

Yaksik
Sweet Rice with Nuts and Jujubes

수
정
과

<u>50</u>

Sujeonggwa

Cinnamon Punch

Serves 6 as a dessert or a cold tea

Ingredients

60 g (2 oz) ginger, peeled and sliced

100 g (3 ½ oz) cinnamon stick

3 litres (3 qts) cold water

1 ½ cups brown sugar

1 dried persimmon

1 tablespoon pine nuts

½ teaspoon salt

Sujeonggwa

Method

수
정
과

1

Put ginger in a pot with 1 ½ liters (1 ½ quarts) of water.
Bring to a boil. Lower the heat and simmer for 30 minutes.

2

Put a cinnamon stick in a pot with 1 ½ liters (1 ½ quarts) of water.
Bring to a boil. Lower the heat and simmer for 30 minutes.

This refreshing punch is a traditional Korean beverage. It is served during the winter holidays such as Lunar New Year's Day. Dark, reddish brown in color, it is made from dried persimmons, cinnamon, and ginger. The drink is often garnish with pine nuts. The aroma of ginger and cinnamon is welcoming and soothing to the soul. The brew can be enjoyed hot or cold.

3

Separately drain the ginger and cinnamon broth in a colander.
Mix together. Add sugar and salt. Let it cool down.

4

Add dried persimmon. Store in the refrigerator until ready to serve.

5

Garnish with pine nuts. Serve cold.

Sujeonggwa

팥
빙
수

<u>51</u>

Patbingsu

Korean Shaved Ice with Sweet Red Bean

Serves 4 as a snack or a dessert

Ingredients

800 g (1 lb 7 oz) shaved ice

2 dried persimmons

2 dried jujubes, julienne

2 tablespoons bean powder, roasted
and largely diced

4 tablespoons sweetened condensed milk
or 1 cup of milk

100 g (3 ½ oz) rice cakes, cut into a bite size

Sauce

Sweet red bean paste

1 cup dried red beans *(adzuki beans)*

6 cups water

1 cup sugar

1 cup honey

½ teaspoon cinnamon powder

½ teaspoon ginger powder

2 teaspoons salt

Patbingsu

Method

팥빙수

1

Rinse dried red beans in a cold water. Soak in water overnight.
Drain. Boil the red beans with 6 cups of water, until fully cooked.
Reserve 2 cups of water with the red beans. Set aside.

2

Add sugar, honey, cinnamon powder, ginger powder and salt to the
cooked red beans. Simmer over low heat until liquid thickens.
Cool and store in the refrigerator.

Tip

Patbingsu is one of the most all time popular summer desserts and snacks in Korea. It looks like a huge snow mountain in a bowl, garnished with colorful fruits, sweet red beans, rice cake pieces, and sweet, creamy condensed milk. When one feels exhausted from the heat in the summer, eating this will make you feel revitalized, while cooling down your body temperature. There are many different variations. You can create your very own unique bingsu with your favorite toppings.

3
Put shaved ice into a bowl.

4
Spoon the chilled red bean paste over the shaved ice.
Add rice cakes, dried persimmons, and jujubes.
Sprinkle roasted bean powder on the top.
Serve it with sweetened condensed milk or milk aside.

호떡

<u>52</u>

Hotteok

Pan-fried Sweet Pancake

Serves 4 as a snack

Ingredients

2 cups bread flour

100 g (3 ½ oz) glutinous rice powder

1 teaspoons dried yeast

1 cup warm water (40ºC 104ºF)

1 tablespoon sugar

½ teaspoon salt

4 tablespoons vegetable oil

Sauce

Filling

70 g (2 ½ oz) mixed nuts, roasted and crushed

100 g (3 ½ oz) dark brown sugar

1 teaspoon cinnamon powder

Hotteok

Method

호떡

1

Dissolve the yeast with 2 tablespoons of warm water in a bowl.
Combine flour, rice powder, and salt with yeast mixture to make
the dough. Knead the dough until the surface becomes smooth.

2

Proof dough for 40 minutes at 40ºC (104ºF)
until the dough rises almost twice its size.

3

In a bowl, combine all the ingredients for the filling.

Tip

Hotteok

4

Put some oil on both palms. Tear off some of the dough. Make the dough into a pocket shape. Put 1 tablespoon of filling in the center. Seal the pocket tightly.

5

Heat oil in a pan. Place the sealed dough to grease one side of dough. After 5 seconds, flip it over. Press down with a spatula. Cook over medium heat until golden-brown. Press several times to evenly cook.

6

Serve immediately.

약
식

<u>53</u>

Yaksik

Sweet Rice with Nuts and Jujubes

Serves 4 as a dessert

Ingredients

2 cups glutinous rice

4 chestnuts, peeled

6 dried jujubes

1 tablespoon pine nuts

Sauce

¾ cup dark brown sugar

2 tablespoons soy sauce

2 tablespoons sesame oil

1 teaspoon cinnamon powder

⅓ teaspoon salt

Yaksik

Method

약
식

1
Soak the glutinous rice in cold water for 3 hours and then drain.

2
Cut the chestnuts into quarters. Remove the seeds
and slice the jujubes. Remove the cones from the pine nuts.

3
Steam the rice for about 50 minutes.

4
Mix all ingredients for the seasoning in a bowl.

Tip

Yaksik is a traditional Korean delicacy. It is eaten either on the first full moon of the lunar calendar, at weddings, or festivities. Yaksik was viewed a medicinal food, for its use of honey as its main ingredient. This delicious dessert goes well with hot tea.

Yaksik

5

Add the seasoning to the steamed rice. Mix well. Let it sit for 30 minutes.

6

Add the chestnuts, jujubes and pine nuts to the steamed rice.
Mix all together.

7

Place rice back into the steamer. Steam it for 50 minutes.

8

Let it cool down. Put the *yaksik* in a mold. After removing the *yaksik*
from the mold, cut into bite-sized pieces. Serve at room temperature.

Index

A

Acorn Jelly Salad	52
Anchovy Stock	22

B

Baechu-kimchi	208
Beef Stock	26
Beoseot-bokkeum	56
Bibim-guksu	84
Bibimbap	186
Bossam	156
Braised Chicken in a Soy Sauce	148
Braised Mackerel	102
Braised Short Ribs	136
Braised Tofu in Soy Sauce	76
Bulgogi	128

C

Chaeso-gimbap	182
Chaeso-yuksu	30
Cinnamon Punch	242
Cooked White Rice	178
Cucumber Kimchi	212
Cucumber Salad	40

D

Dak-galbi	140
Dak-gangjeong	144
Desserts	240
Diced Radish Kimchi	216
Doenjang-jjigae	236
Dotori-muk-muchim	52
Dubu-jorim	76
Dubu-kimchi	228

F

Fermented Foods	206
Fresh Kimchi (Korean Salad)	220
Fried Chicken with Flavored Soy Sauce	144

G

Galbi-gui	132
Galbi-jjim	136
Gamja-sujebi	92
Geot-jeori	220
Ginseng Chicken Soup	152
Godeungeo-jorim	102
Grilled Beef Ribs	132
Gyeran-jjim	168

H

Haemul-pajeon	122
Hobak-juk	194
Hobak-namul	64
Hotteok	250

J

Jaeyuk-bokkeum	160
Japchae	68
Jjim-dak	148

K

Kimchi	208
Kimchi-bokkeum-bap	190
Kimchi-jeon	224
Kimchi-jjigae	232
Kimchi Fried Rice	190
Kimchi Pancake	224
Kimchi Stew	232
Kimchi Wraps with Pork	156
Kkakdugi	216
Kkotge-tang	114
Kong-guksu	89
Kong-namul-muchim	48
Korean Shaved Ice with Sweet Red Bean	246

L

Leaf Wraps and Rice	89

M

Meat Dishes	126
Miyeok-gu	118
Mu-saengchae	44
Mung Bean Pancake	80
Myeolchi-bokkeun	110
Myeolchi-yuksu	22

N

Nokdu-bindae-tteok	80
Noodles in Cold Soybean Soup	88

O

Oi-saengchae	40
Oi-sobagi	212
Ojingeo-bokkeum	106

P

Pan-fried Sweet Pancake	250
Patbingsu	246
Potato Hand-pulled Dough Flakes Soup	92
Pumpkin Porridge	194
Pyogobeoseot-jeon	164

R

Radish Salad	44
Rice Dishes	176

S

Samgyetang	152
Seafood and Green Onion Pancake	122
Seafood Dishes	100
Seasoned Bean Sprouts	48
Seasoned Spinach	60
Seasoned Zucchini	64
Seaweed Soup	118
Shiitake Mushroom Pancake	164
Sigeumchi-namul	60
Silken Tofu Salad	72
Sliced Rice Cake Soup	198

Snacks	240
Soft Tofu Stew	96
So-gogi-yuksu	26
Soybean Paste Stew	236
Spicy Beef Soup	172
Spicy Blue Crab Stew	114
Spicy Noodles	84
Spicy Stir-fried Chicken	140
Ssal-bap	178
Ssam-bap	36
Steamed Eggs	168
Stir-fried Anchovies	110
Stir-fried Assorted Mushrooms	56
Stir-fried Glass Noodles and Vegetables	68
Stir-fried Kimchi with Tofu	228
Stir-fried Pork	160
Stir-fried Rice Cake	202
Stir-fried Squid	106
Sujeonggwa	242
Sundubu-jjigae	96
Sweet Rice with Nuts and Jujubes	254

T

Tteok-bokki	202
Tteokguk	198

V

Vegetable Dishes	34
Vegetable Gimbap	182
Vegetable Stock	30

Y

Yaksik	254
Yeondubu	72
Yukgaejang	172